Sweden: The Middle Way on Trial

Sweden:
The Middle Way
on Trial

MARQUIS W. CHILDS

Yale University Press
New Haven and London
1980

Designed by James J. Johnson
and set in VIP Garamond No. 3 type by
United Printing Services, Inc., New Haven, Conn.
Printed in the United States of America by
Vail-Ballou Press, Binghamton, N.Y.

Published in Great Britain, Europe, Africa, and
Asia (except Japan) by Yale University Press,
Ltd., London. Distributed in Australia and
New Zealand by Book & Film Services, Artarmon,
N.S.W., Australia; and in Japan by Harper & Row,
Publishers, Tokyo Office.

Library of Congress Cataloging in Publication Data

Childs, Marquis William, 1903–
    Sweden, the middle way on trial.

    Bibliography: p.
    Includes index.
    1. Sweden—Economic conditions—1945–
2. Sweden—Economic policy.   3. Industry and state–
Sweden   I. Title.
HC375.C52   330.9′485′05   79-24714
ISBN 0–300–02443–6

To my wife, Jane,
with thanks for
her help and
her patience

Contents

vii

Acknowledgments

I am indebted to so many individuals that it would be a hopeless task to try to thank them. Talks over the years in Sweden with knowledgeable men and women have been the principal basis for this book. But I must express my gratitude to two who have been constantly helpful. One is Leif Leifland, secretary general of the Swedish Foreign Office, who both in Washington, where he served as chargé d'affaire during a difficult time, and in Stockholm has given me wise counsel. The second is Lars Arno, a counselor of the Swedish embassy in Washington, who has been unfailingly patient in responding to repeated inquiries.

I hope the bibliography of the monographs and books I used will be helpful. As in *Sweden: The Middle Way* I have not used footnotes, which may distress academic readers, but I like to think that so unencumbered it will facilitate reading by others. Needless to say I am responsible for whatever errors occur.

I wish to thank Mrs. George W. Hamilton for preparing the manuscript.

I Sweden of the Forests

The long dark sweep of the forest held much of the country in solitude broken only by occasional villages. The people, 90 percent at least, lived off the land, forestry of a primitive sort, and farming. Poor, they nevertheless had a certain independence growing out of the powers of parliament and the "reduction" of the nobles, whose share of the land was less than 40 percent. This was Sweden in the late eighteenth and nineteenth centuries, much of it on a parallel latitude with Alaska, part of it lying beyond the Arctic Circle.

The rugged quality of this northern peninsula has always been a part of my attachment. We stayed in mid-July in a nearly empty ski lodge close to the Norwegian border. On the granite mountains there were still patches of snow. I could hear the echoes of those lines from Shakespeare, during the revels at Elsinore. Old Norway, a sturdy force untouched by the decadence of the Danish court, that was the invocation, the warning for the corrupt king. The sophisticated Sweden, the Sweden of the middle way, was built on that sturdy base with so much of the native root preserved.

Long ago were the days of high adventure when Gustaf II Adolf had invaded Russia, Poland, and Germany, carving out an empire on the rim of the Baltic. Later Vasa kings contended with the powers on the continent and repeatedly did battle with the Danes. Those wars had been

fought by peasant armies. Now the peasants wanted none of it. Lutheranism had come peacefully, a reformation without bloodshed. Queen Christina's conversion to Catholicism, her abdication, and her refuge in Rome was only a brief interruption in the calm flow of existence.

The state Lutheran church had once exercised the primary responsibility for local affairs, including education. But in 1842, with the creation of new communal structures, the church lost much of its secular power. In subsequent decades Lutheran doctrines stressing the obligation of citizens to obey established political authority were challenged by the proliferation of dissenting sects. The importance of religion in the daily life of the average Swede steadily declined. While 90 percent of all citizens are nominal members of the state church, few take part in religious services. According to a survey by Paul Austin, in a Stockholm suburb in 1966 nearly 60 percent of the respondents had not gone to church in years and only 14 percent professed belief in Christian doctrines. Sweden was rapidly becoming a secular state with religious values out of the past permeating the reforms of a secular society.

a secular state

But the importance of the church in the early centuries in establishing the communal nature of Swedish life can hardly be exaggerated. It was the force that through the long dark winters gave a center to life. As much as anything else it was the cohesive stamp in Swedish character. Prior to 1842 the church was the unifier, in a sense the leveler for all the distinctions of title and rank. A stubborn Swede—that was often the judgment on the emigrants to the new world—and that stubborn quality owed not a little to the indoctrination of those shut-away years when the church in the village was the common denominator. This is the spirit that infuses the novels of Selma Lagerlöf.

The solitude—free of invasion, free of war and internal upheaval—shaped the Swedish character. They were alone on a peninsula that for more than half the year, except for the extreme south, was under snow and ice, and in

imp of solitude in shaping Sw. character

the winter a cloud cover obscured the sun for days on end. They tended to be self-centered, self-sustaining, if only by reason of geography. It was a far cry from the Vikings, who raided, pillaged, and traded over much of the fringes of Europe.

A rudimentary form of politics gave an outlet for conflict within the small elite in the cities. The Hats, after military headgear, and the Caps, nightcaps, differed over foreign policy, the former looking to the East, the latter to the West and France. But these were largely theoretical differences, since the government had little power to determine the course of European events. The French influence was important. As it grew, Stockholm, which for the tourist guidebooks is tagged the Venice of the North, took on a sophisticated look that was nevertheless part of the northern and Baltic heritage. It is a tribute to successive city planners that the distinction of the central city, dominated by the massive rosy-gray Italianate royal palace, designed by Tessin, has come down relatively intact.

A curious character, a carrier of the French influence, was Count Axel von Fersen. He built a small baroque palace not far from the Foreign Ministry and adorned its cupolas with gilded ornaments that still glow with light. Spending a great deal of time at the Court of Versailles he became, so the legend is, one of Marie Antoinette's lovers. At any rate he felt that the rumors of his affair were such as to compel him to leave the court, after he had had a leading part in helping to smuggle the royal family from Paris to Varennes, and to join Lafayette in America to fight for the revolution under Washington. His letters from that period give revealing glimpses into the troubles of Washington and his ragged forces. Returning to Sweden he seems to have been branded as a foreigner and a fop with no allegiance to his own country. In 1810 he was beaten and trampled to death by a mob in Stockholm.

This may have been evidence of the fierce determination not to owe any debt to the outside. The Swedes were

self contained, homogeneous

self-contained, and they were to become before the Second World War perhaps the most homogeneous people in the world. The tall blonde Swedes, with some native darker variations, are dominant. With their cool, almost detached air they are a handsome people, the women often beautiful. However, the importation of foreign workers in the years of prosperity after World War II, about 200,000 Finns among others, meant that their homogeneity was not to endure forever.

foreign workers

But at the same time a massive movement was occurring that was part of the great transformation marking the nineteenth century. Between 1840, roughly, and 1930, 1,300,000 Swedes emigrated to North America, the majority to the United States. Wisconsin and Minnesota with their many lakes and forests attracted thousands of newcomers. They were to make a deep imprint on American life, and the ties with the motherland strengthened the relationship between the two countries. Hardly a Swede does not have a relative on the other side of the Atlantic. When Mrs. Karin Söder, foreign minister in the coalition government, came to Washington at the end of June 1977, she held a series of high-level meetings, beginning with Secretary of State Cyrus Vance. But almost as important was the renewal of family ties—a great aunt in Rochester, New York, and cousins in and around Chicago. Many of the new settlers were enraptured with the new world. Frederika Bremer, a novelist famous in her day both in Sweden and the United States, wrote from Charleston, South Carolina, in 1850:

To U.S., 1840–1930

I have been here now fourteen days and though the weather has been mostly rainy (and is so even now) I have still enjoyed days when I have wished that the whole of weak, sickly humanity might be moved here, breathe of this air, see this lovely splendor of sky and earth, that they may recover as by a balm of life and enjoy life anew. I can understand that the seafarers who first approached these

coasts and felt these winds, this air, believed themselves to be drinking an elixir and hoped to find here the fountain of eternal youth.

More than a century later a harsher and a more realistic portrayal of the mass movement from the old world came in two films, *The Emigrants* and *The New World*. With Liv Ullman in the principal role, the start of her international reputation, they were touched with the darkling tragedy that is Sweden's hallmark. They reflected the courage and stoicism with which the settlers faced a world that was alien and often harsh and cruel.

Slowly in Sweden itself changes were taking place. Industrialization was beginning and without the worst of the blight that had characterized the industrial revolution in Britain. The rich reserves of iron ore that were to play an important part in Sweden's future were increasingly developed and at the same time other minerals—gold, lead, and copper—from the mines around Boliden. They had been exploited in primitive fashion for centuries. Two strains were to become important in the development of Sweden to a position of influence in international affairs. The first was the capacity for organization. Both in industry and in government, from the highest level down to the county councils, citizens without number have given themselves to the tasks of organization. The innumerable commissions that have preceded every important reform have meant days, weeks, and months of serious and concentrated effort. Few countries can show a comparable record of solid endeavor often leading the way to compromise and general acceptance of a measure that may have seemed at the outset too radical and innovative. Royal commissions have paved the way for almost every welfare step adopted into law. Often such studies required years before they were ready to be presented to the Riksdag and the public. It was a procedure that almost always brought success except when impatience with the rate of change in a more radical

direction brushed aside this safeguard of transition.

The second factor was education. Compulsory school-ing through the sixth grade came toward the end of the nineteenth century, and this was later extended to the ninth grade. Increasingly the young from blue-collar and lower-middle-class families entered the universities. Literacy is at levels that few other countries—Switzerland possibly—can match. The per capita circulation of books, magazines, and newspapers is phenomenally high. Freedom was highly prized. In 1766 the Riksdag had passed a free press law. This was later expanded to assure access to government documents and government hearings, with eventually a press ombudsman and a press council. The law of 1766 was one of the first of its kind in the West.

Change was coming. For all its geographical remove Sweden could not stay clear of the turmoil of the Napoleonic wars. Recognizing the reality of the struggle on the continent, Sweden entered into alliances with Britain, Russia, and Prussia. With the death of the last of its hereditary kings, Sweden confronted a disquieting gap in the structure of constitutional government. This coincided, as one consequence of the involvement in the struggle on the continent, with the loss of Finland and the exhaustion of the armed forces. In the dilemma the Riksdag voted to elect one of Napoleon's marshals, Jean Bernadotte, as king. When he set foot on Swedish soil in 1810 he became Crown Prince Karl Johan, succeeding to the throne as Charles XIV in 1818. Tending to be repressive toward certain democratic institutions, he caused no little unhappiness among a people who had prized their freedoms. He was succeeded by his more liberal son, Oscar I. It has proved a durable line, accommodating to an ever more symbolic role and helped by a sense of humor. When Gustaf V, who saw his country through two world wars as a neutral, put in on his yacht to a port in the south of France he encountered peasants with the name Bernadotte. He is

supposed to have said to the members of his family who were with him, "There are your cousins living as we would have lived if we had not been elected kings of Sweden."

He was a gracious, outwardly unassuming constitutional monarch. I talked with him in 1943 as he was about to take part in a doubles tennis match. Spare, rather plain in appearance, he had an engaging smile. You are going to see, he said, a very old king play very poor tennis. He was then eighty-five. As a matter of fact he played with an easy skill, all those years on the courts of the Riviera having given his game a comfortable assurance. He lived to the age of ninety-two, leaving his eldest son, the crown prince, leisure to travel in Italy and the Far East, exercise his active interest in archaeology, and put together a splendid collection of Chinese art, most of which he left to the small but marvelously selective museum of Oriental art near the National Museum.

The tide of change sweeping the West was felt with full force in Sweden. Despite stout resistance, trade unions gained a firm hold in the country's leading industries. Then in 1909 a shattering event occurred that was to have consequences for many years. The unions called a general strike, and those employees who did not go out were locked out by the employers. Labor lost this trial of strength, and it was a long time before a working relationship could be established between the two sides with the government as friendly mediator.

In politics as well the yeast of change was at work in the solid Swedish mass. A towering figure was at the outset to lead the way toward a radical transformation of the nation's life. With his sweeping moustachios and his low-keyed but persuasive voice, Karl Hjalmar Branting had formed the Social Democratic party that under his direction in the initial years was to challenge the bourgeois parties.

His father had been a professor of gymnastics who

worked with the handicapped. Conservative medical men were in open opposition to his methods, which were innovative for their time. This caused the elder Branting great distress, and it is thought to have resulted in the alienation of his son from the comfortable middle-class life of a professor's family. In that day, as indeed today, a professorship was highly prized, the source of passionate personal rivalries, and with it go honors and perquisites. Young Hjalmar went to school with the crown prince who was to become King Gustaf V. Certainly if Branting had stayed in line he could have attained a high position in the accepted channels of political life.

But the sweep of radical and even revolutionary ideas had stirred him beyond the safe circumstance into which he had been born. The major influence was that of Karl Kautsky, the leading Marxist theoretician of the German Social Democratic party before World War I. A friend of Friedrich Engels in London, he became after Engels's death in 1895 the principal Marxist theoretician. His thinking was colored by the Social Darwinism of the time, which led him to the conviction that, while the Social Democratic party was revolutionary, it stood for a revolution that was inevitable through a process of evolution. Thus it obviated the need for any violent overthrow, since socialism was certain to come with the passage of time. Needless to say, this "revisionist" Marxism was anathema to Lenin and the Bolsheviks.

While this revisionist Marxism may not have been suited to German Social Democrats, so soon to feel the shattering blow of the First World War, it was well adapted to Sweden and, for that matter, to Branting. He may have flirted with the philosophy of anarchy prevalent at the end of the century, but he was, as he matured, a man of the center. Elected to the lower chamber of the Riksdag for the first time in 1896, he was the only Social Democrat to serve there until 1902.

Branting gave direction to the party as it was to grow in succeeding years. He gathered around him young intellectuals from the universities, most of them of bourgeois origin. They considered themselves socialists, but theirs was essentially a reform socialism. One of the young men was Östen Undén, who became foreign minister in a subsequent Social Democratic government. This was the pattern as the party grew to be the dominant force and the governing power for more than forty years. Although the extent of public ownership was extended with the development of hydroelectric power, these socialists were prepared to cooperate with the owners of private industry, who controlled well over 90 percent of the means of production. As a man of the center, Branting was ready to break with the left wing of his party. Attracted by the example of the Soviet Union, the left socialists began to split off in 1917, and in 1921 they organized the Communist party of Sweden. Branting was careful to cultivate the Liberals, whose strength lay in the middle class, and in 1917 he became minister of finance in a Liberal-Social Democratic coalition. In 1920 he formed Sweden's first Social Democratic government, and though the elections of the following September went against him he formed another government in 1923.

Branting had two principal aims. One was the extension of universal suffrage, which came slowly as landholding requirements were removed. The second and more important was peace and neutrality. In the First World War the three Scandinavian countries were firmly locked in a common determination to stay out of the war. The break between Norway and Sweden in 1905 had come peaceably, thanks in no small part to Branting. With food stocks and other supplies often short, the three nations shared hardships along with a common determination to keep out of the conflict raging on the continent.

The moderate nature of Swedish socialism was epito-

mized by a resolution passed in 1889—Branting was then twenty-eight—at the founding of the Social Democratic party:

Sweden's Social Democratic party in its efforts to organize the Swedish working class for its conquest of political power will make use of such means as correspond to the people's natural sense of justice. The contemporary program which we have formalized and for which we are working is the best proof that we, for our part, are by no means striving for a violent revolution. We expressly refute the foolish plan attributed to us by our enemies that we wish to endanger the entire labor movement by attempting some sort of violent coup without sufficient support by the people. . . . Revolution can never be "made"; but should the blindness of egoism among the ruling classes provoke a violent revolution in self-defense, our place is assigned, and we are prepared to do all that is necessary to help the people secure and preserve as valuable fruits of the battle all that is possible.

Although he suffered from ill health beginning in 1917 he stayed on as leader of his party. At the war's end he became a devoted advocate of the League of Nations. With Undén at his side he spent a great deal of time in Geneva working to strengthen and improve the League. In 1921 he was awarded the Nobel peace prize for his labors for the League. Branting died in February 1925 at the age of sixty-four. He had shaped a powerful political movement, and his image was to be dominant for many years to come.

Sweden was in transition, moving toward the time when the Swedish example could attract the notice of the world. Talents and skills were developed that had been dormant during the long period of isolation. This was enhanced by the prosperity that came shortly after the end of the war. The policy of the government was one of progress by peaceful negotiation. The eight-hour day was intro-

duced, and, although working hours were shorter, production expanded. The merchant fleet was greatly increased, and the production of wood and pulp, spurred by government cooperation with industry in improving forestry and seed selection in agriculture, greatly expanded. Industry developed the specialty high-grade steels that were to be important in the export trade vital to a nation depending on trading abroad to live. Having come through the war unscathed, Sweden was in an excellent position to supply the needs of a ravaged continent.

But it was above all in the arts and crafts that the Swedes showed a new face to the world. The Swedish exhibit, as well as the Danish, at the Paris exposition of 1925 got marked attention. The inventiveness and beauty of Orrefors in glass was a pioneering endeavor to be widely emulated in later years. So was the use of pewter in designs—modern yet nevertheless with a feeling for the north country of its origin. In literature Selma Lagerlöf evoked in her novels the warm and often sentimental past that was nevertheless colored with a sense of the present.

The achievement that marked a kind of renaissance in the arts was the building of the Town Hall. Both literally and figuratively it expressed the hopes and desires of a people liberated from the past. Hundreds of citizens contributed by buying individual copper shingles that were then inscribed with the donors' names. Like everything else in Sweden, the Town Hall was a long time in gestation. In 1908 the Stockholm City Council resolved that a municipal building should be erected, with a committee of seven members appointed to draw up plans.

This committee took a year to complete its task, but because other important municipal building operations were already in progress the project was delayed until 1911 before it was finally settled that the Town Hall should be built on the site directly opposite the old "City within the Bridges" on the cape that juts out between Riddarfjarden and Klaraviken. It was a site admirably

suited to underscore the character of Stockholm as a maritime stronghold. The close proximity of the "City within the Bridges," a walled city in the Middle Ages until Gustavus Vasa crossed the drawbridge to the gate and was given the keys to the city, together with the lively movement on Lake Mälaren and the stream of traffic through Kungsholmen, linked the site with both the old and the new life of the town.

The next step was the selection of an architect. After long deliberation the choice fell on Ragnar Östberg. He had traveled widely in the United States and Europe, and the concept of a city hall had long been in his mind. While still a student he had taken part in discussions about the need for a building that would contain the administrative offices of the city and the courts. In 1893 at the age of twenty-seven he was admitted to an exhibition of city hall projects. His entire life, including his earlier work, had prepared him for the creation of the splendid building that epitomizes so much of the simplicity and the strength of the city.

From the terrace garden on the water to the three golden crowns atop the cupola on the square tower the tone is of life, vitality, that is nevertheless unpretentious and even modest. It is no marble palace but a red brick stronghold that gleams with color in the early morning sunlight. The open court (the Civic Court) and the covered court (the elegant Blue Hall) form in conjunction with the Southern Arcade the three public places around which the various functioning offices of the City Council are built. Under the great projecting timbers of the cornice there are gilded figures in relief. They represent the workers of Stockholm during the 800 years of the existence of the city down to 1923. The thirteenth century is represented by the carpenter, the mason, the bricklayer; the fourteenth by the copyist, the weaver, the accountant; the fifteenth by the glassworker, the wood carver, the warrior; the sixteenth by the coiner, the smith, and the king, Gustavus

Vasa; the seventeenth by the pewterer, the goldsmith, the governor; the eighteenth by the builder, Tessin, at work on the king's palace, the singer, and the artist; the nineteenth by the scientist, the engineer, the politician, Branting; the twentieth by the sister of mercy and the wrestler. The summit of the Maiden Tower is crowned with a group of St. George and the Dragon in bronze, designed by Christian Eriksson, that comes to life when the clock strikes noon and 6 P.M. Leading sculptors and painters did work in stone and the frescoes that adorn the interiors.

Artistic life was coming into being on every hand. The sculptor Carl Milles had begun to win his international reputation. His *The Sun Singer* stands on a small promontory looking across the water to the Grand Hotel and the National Museum. Much of his work is in American museums, and originals or copies stand in the sculpture garden adjoining his house and studio in suburban Lidingö, outside Stockholm. On summer nights, when the sun skirts the horizon at midnight with a curious green dusk, the mythical figures he created seem to come alive with the green patina of the bronze. They are the heirs of the ancient past, the sea creatures rising from the spray of the fountains. In this green twilight, as the creator talked to me of one or the other of his creations, he himself had the look of a fable risen from the sea with the brine still in his thick matted hair. One of his greatest works, *Orpheus*, is placed before the Concert Hall, where each year the Nobel laureates receive their prizes from the king.

A triumph in quite another vein was the first motor ship, *Kungsholm*. The interior decor entirely the work of Swedish artists and artisans, it was one of the most beautiful ships in the Atlantic run, sailing from New York to Gothenburg. The public rooms, with paneling in contrasting woods showing scenes out of the past and with glass used imaginatively, were a celebration of the Swedish revival. On a tide of prosperity, both from the luck of the

day with a continent rebuilding and Germany rearming, and from the shrewd fiscal management of the Social Democrats coupled with the innovative direction of rapidly expanding industry, Sweden was on the way to a stature in the world undreamed of when farmers and foresters lived in a remote northern peninsula. Here was a nation with a population of eight and a half million that was to build and market two motor cars and several airplanes, including a supersonic jet. Swedish organizing ability, Swedish ingenuity, Swedish pride were all part of this long stride into the future.

2 *Road Map to the Middle Way*

The depression that followed the end of the First World War affected Sweden profoundly. At one point in the twenties, as the worldwide depression deepened, from a third to a half of the Swedish labor force was unemployed. Conflict between the Socialists and the bourgeois parties came to a head in the campaign preceding the election of 1928.

The right exploited the concern of the electorate over bolshevism and socialization. This concern had grown with the sponsorship by the Social Democrats of a radical inheritance tax and the formal cooperation of the party with the Communists. The debate took on a rancor rare in Swedish politics as the right-wing parties raised the specter of nationalization and the end of democracy. In the second chamber elections that year, the Social Democrats suffered their greatest losses up to that time. A Conservative government replaced the minority government of the Prohibitionist party.

In the wake of this disaster two men were to lead the party out of the pit of defeat. One was Per Albin Hansson, sturdy, plainspoken, in appearance a typical working-class Swede who had served faithfully and well in the ranks of the Social Democrats. In the years he was prime minister he was without pretension, riding the street car to and from his office in the chancellery. At the same time he did not hesitate to tell his colleagues where he thought they

15

had gone wrong and why in his opinion they had suffered such a disastrous loss. He let the trade unions, the party's close ally, know where they had exceeded their writ and in so doing had alienated public opinion. His round beneficent face was to become for millions of his countrymen an assurance of peace and prosperity. Per Albin, known to young and old alike by his familiar name, was to be the archetype of the moderate socialist leader with the well-being of his country as well as his party at heart.

The second figure, Ernst Wigforss, was in many ways Per Albin's opposite. An intellectual, an ideologue, he was to give a new direction to the party and to Sweden's economy. At the University of Lund, Wigforss studied Scandinavian languages, and he later became an assistant professor in this field, publishing a book about the dialects spoken in southern Halland. Although he turned to economics and fiscal policy, language was an interest that was to continue throughout his long life. Studying economics and the "science" of fiscal management, he also covered the literature of Marxism, though never becoming a convinced Marxist himself.

An active Social Democrat during his years at Lund, he quickly rose in the party's ranks after his graduation. Witty, brilliant, with an absorbing interest in the people of every kind and class, he was to become a kind of Social Democratic saint as the years passed. No figure in the country's political life was so hotly debated and roundly denounced by conservatives as Wigforss. As a true socialist he believed that capitalism, with competition as the guiding force, meant squandering resources. Unemployment wasted human capacities and was a humiliation of the individual. This conviction was at the base of the policies he carried out in the thirties. But at the same time he opposed the forces that "want to put all economic power in the hands of a centralized public administration."

A member of parliament in 1919, he became minister

of finance at the age of forty-four in 1925. But his two years as finance minister at that time were only a rehearsal for his assumption of that office six years later, and he then served from 1932 to 1949. In addition to his own belief in Keynesian economics he drew on the theories of Gunnar Myrdal, the distinguished Swedish economist who received the Nobel prize for economics in 1977, and Bertil Ohlin, for many years the leader of the Liberal party. Ohlin was to say that Wigforss never had an opportunity to realize the Keynesian theory of economic recovery in full scale. One reason was a series of conflicts in the labor market. And later, with the draft during the Second World War and a great increase in the number of men in uniform, a labor policy was of course superfluous. In the wartime coalition Wigforss was one of the four Social Democratic members who wanted to refuse Germany the right to send German troops through Sweden to Finland. Logical, scholarly, almost pedagogical in political debate, Wigforss saw the chairmanship of his party pass not to him but to Per Albin.

The two men, Hansson and Wigforss, were at opposite poles. The tensions between them never went beyond the bounds of friendship between colleagues and allies, and they contributed to the vitality, the creativeness, and the success of the party. It was not polarization so much as the kind of political dialogue that gives meaning to political change.

The first important step toward the middle way was taken in 1930, when the Social Democrats proposed in the Riksdag under the sponsorship of Wigforss abolishing the entire work relief system and replacing it by productive state work at wages set by contract. In the next two years Wigforss pushed through a whole series of Keynesian measures, including state employment for the jobless and support loans for small-scale farmers. In the fall of 1931 Sweden left the gold standard, yet it seemed impossible to

Factors in stability in Sweden (handwritten annotation)

socialist-agrarian partnership (handwritten annotation)

break the declining economic trend. At the end of the year approximately one-fourth of all union workers were unemployed.

But a political alliance was formed between the Farmers party and the Social Democrats. They agreed on mutual support of their respective policies—the farmers backing the Keynesian program for the cities, while the socialists supported loans and other measures to revive the sagging agricultural sector. In the election of 1932 the right-of-center parties took heavy losses, and the gains of the Social Democrats were sufficient to form a coalition government with the agrarians. Per Albin was prime minister and Wigforss minister of finance in the new government, giving them a broad base for further innovations looking to recovery.

Sweden was the first industrialized nation to employ Keynesian measures and on a scale sufficient to make the difference between continuing decline and reviving prosperity. As late as 1939 Sweden was the only country to put a compensatory public works policy into practice on more than a tentative trial and error basis. In the words of one student of Swedish policy, "The Swedish Social Democrats were the first socialist party in the world to be able to increase gradually the power of the state in economic life without revolution or large-scale nationalization."

The socialist-agrarian partnership was the solid foundation on which the reforms of future years were based. Unemployment insurance, expanded old-age pensions, health insurance, housing, the whole gamut of the enlarged welfare state was grounded in a political alliance that was to survive the Second World War. It was the source of the strength of one Social Democratic government after another—a harmonious society moving to correct inequalities of income and standard of living.

The political partnership between the socialists and the farmers was paralleled by an economic partnership between labor and industry, underwritten by the pact of

labor & industry (handwritten annotation)

Saltsjobaden. Agreed to in 1938, after lengthy negotiation between the two sides in the suburban town of Saltsjobaden on the shores of the archipelago leading to the Baltic, it was a bulwark insuring production interrupted by a minimum of strikes and strike threats. Here was a mutual recognition of the accepted roles of the two principals in the economic process, each motivated by a sense of well-being of a country dependent on sales abroad to live. The pact of Saltsjobaden was the key element on which the middle way was based. So long as the international competitiveness of industry, privately owned up to 90 or 95 percent, continued to increase, with prosperity thereby sustained, the growing scope of welfarism could be supported through taxation that tended to keep pace with welfare benefits. A highly disciplined and comprehensive labor movement, blue-collar workers in the umbrella of the Labor Organisationen (the Confederation of Trade Unions, often referred to as LO) and white-collar workers in two unions of their own, was an important element in the stability of the country. So were the tax laws allowing industry to retain a large share of profits tax free for rapid reinvestment. In this way the development of Sweden's high technology was assured.

Another factor in stability was the Labor Court. Instituted in 1929, it was a nonpolitical tribunal of last resort for the unions and industry. But it was also open to individuals seeking redress for what they claimed to be wrongs either by a union or by an employer. With the certainty of an impartial decision for one party or the other, the two sides tended to settle their disputes without recourse to the court. The court was a model for other Scandinavian countries.

As the Keynesian measures took hold and unemployment declined, the concept of a middle way came into being. The world seemed to face a choice between fascism and communism, and Sweden as a laboratory of social and rational democratic decision-making could conceivably of-

fer an alternative to the two violent extremes. I remember on an early visit to Sweden in connection with my first book I came from Germany where the loud and angry evidence of the Nazi uprising was everywhere. The contrast with the peace and serenity of Sweden was striking. A conscientious and highly organized people were working not only through measures by the state but in producer and consumer cooperatives to shape a new and more humane society.

The cooperative movement was an important part of the middle way as I saw it forty years ago. Albin Johansson had been the moving spirit behind the organization of cooperative stores in the principal cities, with the goal of breaking the price monopoly of private retailers. A large element of idealism went into the efforts of hundreds of cooperators to maintain high standards in handsomely designed shops. But there was also the constantly watchful eye and guiding genius of Johansson, exercised through the central organization, Kooperativa Forbundet (KF). He would have been highly successful in whatever line of business he had entered.

As the movement expanded, the goal was to break the hold of cartels on certain household necessities. One was electric light bulbs. A cartel controlled prices throughout Europe, with General Electric a participant in the United States. KF, already supplying a wide variety of services to the individual stores, began to formulate plans for a light bulb factory. Word of this brought an immediate threat from the cartel of a price war. Undeterred, KF used reserve funds to build the Luma plant outside Stockholm. Cooperators in Britain were able to buy a part of the production, and the price of light bulbs in Europe quickly dropped. This was action not by government but by individuals working together in a common interest.

Since then the movement has grown enormously. Today there are 1.9 million family members, which is equiva-

lent to nearly half the population. KF bought a large department store, PUB, in Stockholm. Today a subsidiary organization, DOMUS, directs the operation of 150 department stores around the country. Specialized shops in shoes and clothing have grown up. Large self-service food stores are patterned after those in America, KF having sent specialists over to study the successful operation of such shops. Laboratories and test kitchens have been established to try to insure the cooperative consumer high quality at the lowest cost, and there is a working relationship with the government consumer organization.

Parallel with this development is the success of certain KF business enterprises. One of the most remarkable is in cash registers and other calculating machines. The KF cash register is said to have 12 percent of the world market, with sales offices in cities around the world. Acting for the cooperatives of Scandinavia, the organization is the largest single coffee buyer, with buying agents in a half-dozen countries in Latin America and Africa. Automobile tires are an important manufacture, with production in excess of the needs for Swedish cooperators sold to other cooperatives. A separate organization, OK, started originally as a buying organization for cab owners and others using their own cars professionally, has played an important part in bringing down the cost of private motoring for cooperative members.

All this has meant the investment of large amounts of capital, and it has brought KF in recent years to a radical change. Outside capital is being sought not from the private money market but from pension, union, and other funds of a semipublic nature. These will presumably be cooperative arrangements different in character from the standard interest-bearing loan in private commerce. That is, nevertheless, as derogators of the cooperative movement like to say, big business. Where, they ask, is the idealism that was the inspiration for the movement in its ori-

rel'p with
unions

gins? This is a troubling question to those who realize what a large part idealism played in the beginning of the cooperative movement.

Cooperators are proud of their close relationship with the trade unions and stress particularly the ties between the two movements. A leading article with the title "There Is an Alternative Society," by Per Ahlstrom, editor of *Metalarbetaren*, published in 1976 by the metal workers union, the numerically largest member of LO, was widely circulated. Hailing the ninetieth anniversary of the union, to be celebrated in ten cities, the author observed that the anniversary should remind members of the union that theirs is not the only organization "fighting for a better life for workers."

The union celebration was arranged in collaboration with the principal cooperative enterprises. Ahlstrom listed the way these enterprises had contributed to bettering the life of the workers. Thanks to Folksam, the cooperative insurance group, even those with low wages could afford insurance, thereby improving their personal security. Through HSB, the cooperative housing organization, housing costs had been drastically lowered. In fighting the private oil companies, OK had performed the same service as the cooperative stores had at the start of the movement in breaking retail price monopolies. The travel organization, Reso, had brought vacation travel within reach of almost all. The article listed the benefits offered by the union as well as by the cooperatives and concluded:

The labor movement is multilegged. The Scandinavian labor movement is unique because it managed to create an alternative to a privately owned purely capitalist society. One can live one's life almost entirely within the labor and cooperative movements. If more workers discovered the worth of our brother organizations the labor movement would grow in strength and we would be closer to liberation from the craving for profit of private capitalism.

An important aspect of the middle way is the dedication of citizens, not only officials but at the volunteer
level, to a broad spectrum of reforms. Few peoples accept
their civic responsibilies with the earnest dedication of the
Swedes. They are actively concerned, and often directly involved, with prison reform and crime, alcoholism, mental
health, and the variety of ills that plague a prosperous ur-
banized society.

volunteers

The deeply held Swedish belief, transcending ideological differences, is that the ills of a free society can be
cured, that injustice is intolerable. This is not so much a
matter of doctrine—the certainty of the perfectability of
man, as in the communist world—as a pragmatic belief
acknowledging the frail nature of the human condition.
This is at the root of what has happened in Sweden since
1930. A new government to the right of center in the
1970s had the same motivation as earlier governments to
the left of center. Continuing reform might be slowed by a
financial crisis, but it would be assumed that this was a
passing interruption.

real hope

Wherever you look in the West, and particularly in
the United States, the horrors of overcrowded prisons as
schools for crime are not only a blight on society but a constant threat to the safety of the communities in which those
prisons exist. It was a foregone conclusion in Sweden,
given the conscience of a welfare state, that the penal system should be the object of reform.

penal reform

Swedish prison reform is a striking example of what a
determined and informed effort can do to create a more or
less open system in which either work at the same wage
that would be paid on the outside, study, or, at the prison-
er's option, doing nothing at all is the choice in most institutions. The crime rate tripled in Sweden in fifteen years,
going from 270,000 reported crimes in 1960 to 755,000 in
1975. Most of these are, by American standards, comparatively minor crimes. In all of Sweden there are about 70
homicides a year, including murder and manslaughter.

*the options
in prison*

*crime in
Sweden*

That compares with 1,500 in New York City, which has about the same population as Sweden, and 800 in Detroit. It is illegal in Sweden to carry a hand gun, and permits for rifles and shotguns are difficult to get. Authorities say, however, that acquiring a hand gun illegally is easy. But Swedes simply do not shoot each other. If an officer shoots at an offender, it is the cause of a national investigation.

On a given day the Swedish National Correctional Administration is responsible for about 2,600 inmates and about 600 people awaiting trial. In a thorough study of the Swedish prison system in 1978, Michael S. Serrill, executive editor of the magazine *Corrections* and an authority on American prisons, observed that the basic reform has been the development of small institutions to hold small numbers of prisoners. In most countries 2,600 prisoners would be confined in at best six prisons. In Sweden they are held in 72 separate institutions, and another 19 hold the 600 awaiting trial. Of the two large prisons in Sweden one is Kumla, with 435 beds, about 200 miles west of Stockholm—a high security institution holding international drug smugglers and others considered high escape risks. The other is Osteråker, which was begun by the Correctional Administration and only half finished when it was stopped by a prison reform movement condemning it as just another "prison factory."

The reform movement has followed a course similar to so much of the political development of the late sixties and early seventies. In the fall of 1966 several hundred lawyers, psychiatrists, social workers, and former prison inmates gathered in the town of Strömsund to form an organization called the National Swedish Association for Penal Reform, known by its acronym KRUM. As Michael Serrill observed in his analysis of Sweden's crime and punishment, the system has never been the same since. With an outburst of speeches and press releases KRUM attacked the proposed large-scale building program of the

Correctional Administration. This was immediately taken up in the media and the Riksdag. One result was that prison construction initiated when it appeared that the prison population seemed certain to boom was stopped dead. Osteråker, halted half way through construction, has been in a sense a crippled institution. While its long dark tunnels are lightened by murals done by art students from the area, with the help of inmates, and while prisoners receive all privileges of the reform program, it remains an anomaly between past and present. Smaller institutions, many of them open, followed, thanks in large part to the continuing efforts of KRUM.

Having started out as an apolitical organization, KRUM devoted itself to counseling inmates and former inmates. Its members worked for such goals as an expansion of the indeterminate sentence. But in 1970 the organization became radicalized, with political goals paralleling the leftist trend within LO and the Social Democratic party. It struck out against a "class society which through unequal distribution of power and opportunity contributes to the creation of groups (prisoners, mental patients, drug addicts) socially, economically and culturally expelled." The goal must be the total abolition of imprisonment.

As a step on the way KRUM began to organize prison inmates to agitate for the reduction of the prison population and loosening of controls on inmate behavior. KRUM members began holding study group meetings with prisoners, who had been generally disorganized and apathetic. It was not long before the inmates took matters into their own hands and a hunger strike began at Osteråker. The first collective protest in recent Swedish prison history, it may have sounded mild to Americans long familiar with prison riots suppressed by violence with large-scale casualties and extensive damage, but inmates in thrity-five other prisons were soon striking in sympathy until their number reached 2,000. They were demanding inmate councils in every prison and a system of negotiations on a

nationwide basis between a prisoners' council and the national prison administration. The administration's reply was that most of the demands could not be met without a new law and much larger appropriations. With recurring hunger strikes for two years, the prisoners gained increasing support in the press and within the Riksdag.

Drawing on reports by various government commissions as well as the extensive proposals put forward by the inmates, the Riksdag in April 1974 passed the Act on Correctional Treatment in Institutions. In the introduction it declared that "inmates shall be treated with respect for their human dignity. They shall be treated with understanding for the special difficulties connected with a stay at any institution." Far more than a declaration of intent, the act revolutionized the penal system with the goal of keeping prisoners out of confinement in institutions and once confined to offer every opportunity to align them with the outside world. A distinction was established between "national" and "local" institutions, with those serving under a year assigned to a local prison near their homes. They were given the right during the day to leave the prison for study or work, to engage in recreational activities, or to prepare with housing and a job for their ultimate release. A system of "short furloughs," usually a weekend leave, was provided in the reform act, and as many as 26,000 such furloughs are granted each year. The escape rate is high, and at any given time as many as 400 inmates may have failed to return from furlough.

As revolutionary as these and a host of other reforms must seem, two institutions have, by American standards, an even more radical look. One is Tillberga prison, 120 miles west of Stockholm, where inmates are paid the going local wage of 60 cents to $1 an hour for work or study tax free. They build prefabricated houses, which are sold through a state agency with offices in twenty cities. Half the eighty inmates may be working at house building while the others are employed in a machine shop making metal

products for the state or in the prison kitchen or in maintenance tasks.

Equally remarkable is what is in effect a kind of resort operated by the Correctional Administration at Gruvberget in central Sweden. This was formerly a company town owned by a timber firm which the administration bought and has made available to inmates under long-term sentences who want to get away from confinement in a "prison factory." They have their families or girl friends with them in what in effect is an open "local" institution. Stores and shops add to the sense of a resort community.

As might be expected, these reforms—so many small institutions with so many employees—are very expensive, and that is an aspect that has recently come under close scrutiny and even sharp criticism as the economic crisis has deepened. The daily cost for an inmate averages $75, more than $27,000 a year. The annual budget of the Correctional Administration to maintain the system as reformed is $160 million.

The cost for each individual in the eighteen delinquent centers is higher. Run by the National Board of Health and Welfare, a staff of more than a thousand care for 475 young people between the ages of fifteen and eighteen. This means $100 to $120 a day per "pupil," as they are known, or $36,000 to $43,000 a year. Five of the institutions are coed, and the young are free to pair off as they please, with the girls given the pill and other forms of contraception. If at times there are errors the answer is abortion. Some of the eighteen institutions have locked units where life is more restricted, but no youth may be kept in such a unit for more than two months.

Does this permissive treatment result in rehabilitation for the young offenders? National Board specialists are frank to say no. Most of the "pupils" come from broken homes with parents who are alcoholics or drug addicts. They have been in as many as ten foster homes. Of the total, 80 percent end up in adult jails—they cannot be kept

in delinquent centers after the age of eighteen—in mental hospitals, or on the dole for the rest of their lives. But at least we help 20 percent, the health board specialists say.

Nor are the humane prisons under Sweden's system any assurance that adult prisoners once released will not again lapse into crime. The overall rate of recidivism, defined as any new conviction carrying a penalty greater than a fine, ranges from 15 to 33 percent for first offenders and from 48 to 86 percent for those with previous convictions. The highest rates are for those sentenced to youth prisons and internment—86 percent and 79 percent respectively.

The administration of justice is far more expeditious in Sweden than in the United States. Prolonged appeals pending sentencing or after sentence has been pronounced are practically unheard of. Scandinavians regard the American bail system as abhorrent. It means that the rich get their liberty, while the poor stay in jail. In one respect the approach is stern. Individuals charged with serious crimes such as homicide are kept in isolation pending trial. Association with other prisoners could, the belief is, lead to steps by the accused to prepare his defense under the influence of his cellmates. The period before trial on charges of serious crime is brief.

During a given year 11,000 individuals receive prison sentences. In light of Sweden's liberalized system of justice this seems a large number. But the fact is that nearly half this number are statistics in another deeply rooted reform. They have been sentenced for driving under the influence of alcohol; against the long background of Sweden's teetotaling movement this is considered a serious crime. Drivers with the slightest indication of alcohol in the event of even a minor traffic incident will be subjected to a blood test and are likely to be charged with driving under the influence of drink. I have observed how carefully the injunction against driving while having anything alcoholic is

Alcohol in
Sweden

observed. In a group dining together in the beautiful res-
taurant of Opera Cellaren, the one who will drive after din-
ner touches not so much as a drop of wine.

The Swedes were a hard-drinking people. At the turn
of the century they consumed ten gallons of alcoholic in-
toxicants, largely brannvin (potato brandy) per capita a
year. The climate, the long, cold, dark winters, had something to do with this, as did the Nordic temperament, a
predilection for gloomy introspection. On the other side
were the temperance forces aligned in a political party that
drew sufficient votes in the early years of the century to
have a place in the government. Under an emergency de-
cree all spirits were banned in the general strike of 1909.
The results seemed to be so salutary that the teetotalers initiated a drive for permanent prohibition. It quickly took
hold, and in a voluntary plebiscite 1,884,298 votes were
cast for prohibition and only 16,718 in opposition.

Characteristic of the moderation that has so often prevailed at this point a persuasive advocate stepped forward
to urge a reform rather than the arbitrary imposition of total prohibition. Typically, too, the government named a
commission of eleven to study the liquor question. The
moderate reformer, Dr. Ivan Bratt, was a minority of one
on that commission. Beginning with a series of forceful articles in *Dagens Nyheter* he brought the commission around
to his own view. A beginning had been made in the
Gothenburg plan, which abolished the old-fashioned sa-
loon and transferred the sale of spirits by the glass to restaurants. The manufacture of brannvin was restricted to
certain private companies, with dividends limited by law
and the balance going to the state.

Bratt built on the Gothenburg plan, with the conviction that essential to control of liquor was "disinterested
management." He formed a charter company to replace
the old Stockholm System Company, which had had sole
rights over distribution of liquor. Thanks to prohibitionists

[handwritten margin notes: Bratt system passbook to buy liquor]

on the town council his company was approved and the way was open for application of what became known as the Bratt system.

Control was to be exerted on the individual. In February 1914 the citizens of Stockholm were told that no one would be allowed to buy any form of liquor until he or she had obtained a pass book from the Stockholm System. The citizen applying for a pass book, a *motbok*, was required to state his age, occupation, capital, income, size of family, and record and reputation for sobriety very much as though he were applying for a life insurance policy or a license to drive a car. Implied, as with a license for operating a car, is the same sense of social responsibility.

[handwritten margin note: passbook failed]

In 1954 the Riksdag enacted new liquor control measures that were to become law the following year. It was felt that the pass book system had failed to bring down the level of alcoholic consumption. If you were allowed a certain number of liters a month you seemed to feel that you must consume that amount. I noted that reliance was placed on high prices for all alcoholic beverages and the work of a series of voluntary organizations that received help from the government. Initially the revenue from the high taxes on hard liquor, wines, and beer went to the Ministry of Defense. This gave rise to jokes about having to drink up another bottle of schnapps so that Sweden could afford another gun for the army.

[handwritten margin note: '46-'79 doubled]

That was changed so that the alcohol tax became part of the general revenue. It is today more than 5 percent of the state's income from every source. Demonstrably the pass book system had failed of its objective. Between 1946 and 1975 the consumption of alcohol, measured 100 percent by weight, nearly doubled, going from four liters a person to eight. The total amount spent on alcoholic beverages in 1975 was close to $2 billion. On schnapps the tax is 90 percent of the retail price, 60 percent on heavy foreign wines.

Government commissions and a multiplicity of organ-

izations, both voluntary and embodied in law, work to bring this down. Under the Temperance Act of 1954 problem drinkers may be sent to a public institution for the care of alcoholics. At one point in 1974 a thousand individuals were committed for psychiatric treatment. But the repressive nature of the enforcement provisions of the law was widely criticized, and the likelihood was for a change putting it in the context of a social problem.

While the stress is on the voluntary aspect of treatment and cure, resistance to treatment and repeated drunkenness still bring the individual under compulsory care. This is particularly true with the young who are habitual abusers. Two laws cover compulsion. One is a law on the provision of closed psychiatric care in certain cases. The other, providing for youthful offenders, comes under the Child Welfare Act.

At least a half-dozen voluntary organizations have in recent years received increasing help from the government. Among them are that old familiar, Alcoholics Anonymous; a national organization for problem drinkers with the acronym **ALRO**; Verdandi, a temperance organization for manual workers; and the Temperance Movement of the Christian Churches. As with all reforms, government commissions over the years have repeatedly studied the alcohol problem and have come up with a variety of recommendations. In 1965 so-called medium-strong beer, 3.6 percent of alcohol by weight, was introduced and the sale allowed outside the stores of the System Company. It was soon discovered that the young took to strong beer in quantity, with a resulting marked rise in drunkenness. This precipitated a lenghty debate in the Riksdag and the mass media—a debate that was often acrimonious within the temperance movement. In 1977 medium-strong beer was abolished, and today only beer of a content of 2.8 percent can be sold outside the System stores.

The System stores carefully monitor all purchasers of alcoholic beverages. They have blacklists of the names of

*as much as
a yr. for DUI*

*Drug
Abuse*

those guilty of an alcoholic offense. Laws governing driving while under the influence have in recent years been made much sterner. Drunkenness while driving is an offense that can bring a prison sentence of as much as a year although, according to the Swedish Council on Alcohol and Other Drugs, there could be mitigating circumstances. Revocation of the license of a driver convicted of drunkenness or "insobriety" while driving follows a conviction. Licenses are issued by county authorities. Application for a new license must under normal circumstances await the lapse of a year of good behavior, and at times this is extended to two years. Under the Road Traffic Offenders Act the number of persons charged with driving while under the influence of alcohol has held fairly steady from 1973 through 1976 at about 11,500 a year.

Drug abuse has been on the increase in Sweden. One reason is believed to be the growing number of foreign workers, with an increase in smuggling rings tapping connections in, for example, Turkey, where hashish and heroin are more readily available. The law prohibits and penalizes the possession, offering for sale, transfer, and importation of narcotic drugs except for medical and scientific use.

A thorough fact-finding study made in 1967 showed that there were about 10,000 narcotics abusers. The group consisting of severe abusers, including the far-out mainliners, is thought not to have increased in the intervening years. Many of the young have experimented with pot, although the best evidence is that this is temporary and the experiment given up after a certain age. In 1968 the Riksdag expanded the drug addict law—a special penal law on narcotics and control of imports of syringes and hypodermic needles. In a ten-point program the government got tough with narcotics crimes. Police and customs officers were given increased resources and their cooperation with authorities in Europe broadened. Wiretapping subject to court order was authorized for suspects. But most impor-

tant, penalties were tightened, with a ten-year sentence for a grave narcotic offense, which made it one of the most serious crimes under Swedish law.

At the same time both the education and treatment programs were expanded. As with extreme instances of alcoholism, coercion can be used in recalcitrant cases. But the stress was on a voluntary approach. Extended therapy, above all group therapy, and psychiatry employed to a large extent in the treatment centers tended to show that the irresolution and pessimism of the past about the cure of drug addicts were not justified; there has been a growing confidence in rehabilitation. Currently drug abusers can be treated in some fifteen outpatient wards, more than 100 beds in the drug addict wards of hospitals, and twenty treatment and boarding homes with 230 beds. The centers are kept small with no more than twelve patients. And as with alcoholism, voluntary help is important. The largest organization is RFHL, the National Union for Help to Addicts, with offices in twenty-five towns.

types of treatment

The capacity for organization and dedication to the general good that characterize the Swedish approach to problems such as prison reform, the administration of justice, alcoholism, and drug abuse are evident also in the creative and fairminded way the Swedes have coped with other aspects of life in a modern industrial democracy. Examples are energy use, boredom on the assembly line, helplessness of the citizen in the face of government bureaucracy, and freedom of the press—all have come in for special treatment as part of the middle way. I discuss them here as illustrations.

Other areas

Without oil or coal of its own, Sweden must explore all means of economical fuel use and conservation. For every dollar of gross national product, Sweden uses only 68 percent as much energy as the United States. And if allowance is made for the energy essential for production for the export market, the Swedish figure is 61 percent.

Energy use

Part of this is due to careful planning by the govern-

ment; planning is not a word the Swedes fear. Building codes have been far more carefully drawn to stop heat loss, with double glazing of windows required, for example. Under the codes only energy-efficient and economic construction has been permitted. With a colder climate, Swedish homes, both apartment units and single-family dwellings, are heated to three or four degrees under the level in the United States. In industry, too, tax incentives and careful management have brought substantial economies. After the 1973-74 oil embargo Volvo was able to cut its energy use 25 percent.

One of the principal reasons for the difference in energy use is that lightweight cars are used almost without exception. Weight alone accounts for a 30 percent difference in energy consumption per mile. This is coupled with the lack of power extras such as automatic transmission, power brakes, power steering, and air conditioners, and the lower ratio of engine displacement to car weight. An important reason for light cars is the fact that excise taxes and yearly fees rise with increased weight.

Mass transportation is a major reason for lower energy use in Sweden. In Stockholm, Malmo, and Gothenburg, where more than a quarter of Sweden's population resides, mass transit, motor bikes, and pedal bikes account for 75 percent of all commuting. For the entire country the figure is 46 percent. Most cities of more than 50,000 have bus systems and economic incentives, including subsidies, to encourage their use. During peak hours, buses are often as close as four minutes apart, and direct service to places as far as thirty miles from city centers is provided by rapid rail and bus.

The state-owned Swedish railway system has been efficiently maintained. The use of rail and bus service has brought about the development of garden suburbs for commuters, who find mass transportation an easy and viable way to reach the center of the city. High parking fees are a disincentive for the commuter by automobile.

Intercity buses and trains carry 20 percent of the passenger miles in trips over thirty-five miles. The efficiency and convenience that the railways offer make travel desirable. Swedish Railways has hourly departures between Malmo, Gothenburg, and Stockholm during the day and early evening hours on trains traveling from 60 to 75 miles an hour.

In a detailed analysis of Sweden's methods for saving energy the magazine *Science* concluded that the Swedish economy performs well as an energy-efficient economy. The analysis was completed before the tripling of oil prices, and this has brought about more intensive efforts at conservation. Energy conservation, the study suggests, can actually bring greater well-being for every unit of fuel used rather than any decline in living standards.

In every industrialized society a continuing concern is over the boredom, the repetitive quality, the mindless anonymity of most tasks in large-scale industry. It is expressed in satire, as in Charlie Chaplin's *Modern Times*, and in an endless stream of research into the consequences of deadening day-to-day work on one version of the assembly line or another. One of Sweden's most enlightened and remarkable industrialists, Pehr G. Gyllenhammar, president of Volvo, initiated a new type of plant and work system designed to provide greater incentive and satisfaction as well as greater efficiency in the assembly of a motor car.

The motivation came out of the consequences of new assembly line techniques applied by Volvo in the 1950s and 1960s as plants were overhauled and modernized. Method–time measurement systems were widely used to get increased productivity and greater utilization of production resources. For individual workers this meant constant changes in the working environment. For some the work was less physically demanding, but for others with more rigid attachment to assembly lines it was more burdensome even though the overhaul had meant better lighting and ventilation. A rapid turnover of personnel was

disturbing, as was a high rate of absenteeism and the difficulty of recruiting new workers.

Against this background, the search for new assembly methods began. With typical Swedish deliberation, days of discussion between industrial engineers, supervisors, and union representatives occurred before a decision was reached on the nature of a new plant at Kalmar. The setting for these discussions was Volvo's old car assembly plant at Gothenburg. As Gyllenhammar expressed it:

At Kalmar the objective is to organize automobile production is such a way that employees can find meaning and satisfaction in their work. This is a factory that, without any sacrifice of efficiency or financial results, will give employees the opportunity to work in groups, to communicate freely, to shift among work assignments, to vary their pace, to identify themselves with the product, to be conscious of responsibility for quality and to influence their own work environment. When a product is manufactured by workers who find their work meaningful, it will inevitably be a product of high quality.

Production at Kalmar began in February 1974 with 636 employees—540 blue collar, the balance white collar. Designed to turn out 30,000 cars, the assembly plant is made up of a series of stations each manned by a team of fifteen or twenty. As it is put together with components, engines, axles, and gear boxes supplied by other Volvo operations, the chassis is moved from station to station. There are six functional councils—two for production, one for materials, one for quality, one for industrial engineering, and one for personnel and finance. They serve as a forum where problems of various kinds can be examined, discussed, and solved. Employees are represented on the councils through their unions. In every team area there is a computer terminal with a closed-circuit TV screen giving information on production and quality.

In characteristically Swedish fashion, after two years

of operation a Rationalization Council made up of representatives of the Employers Confederation (SAF) and the Labor Organisationen carried out a thorough analysis of the Kalmar experiment. It was a radical experiment. Each team had its own territory, its own small workshop in the plant. The teams had separate changing rooms and separate coffee rooms. The Rationalization Council concluded after extensive interviews:

Almost without exception workers felt very favorable about working in groups. They noted particularly the feeling of unity, and the tolerance shown by team members for each other. A positive rating was also given to the independence of operation made possible by the team operation. This was true despite the basically close interdependence of the various sections in the plant, stemming from a common materials handling system and the limited capacity of buffers.

felt plus on the groups

On efficiency the Rationalization Council concluded that Kalmar was equal to or better than Volvo's conventional assembly lines. While the plant represented an investment 10 percent greater than a conventional plant, the investigators for the council concluded that this was somewhat offset by production advantages, such as a smaller number of supervisors, ease of altering production arrangements, and low absenteeism and turnover. These advantages were even more marked when Kalmar went into full production.

Although it is a country of only 8,000,000, Sweden has two companies that make trucks and passenger cars. The second one is Saab-Scania, which normally has 34,000 employees and is the third largest company in the country. Under the stimulus in the fifties and sixties of the drive for greater job satisfaction and enrichment, Saab-Scania introduced in its plant at Sodertalje, not far from Stockholm, a team system of assembly not unlike that at Kalmar. By one estimate 500 work places or more in Sweden,

*Saab —
Sania
Scania*

Norway, and Denmark are engaging in work enlargement or enrichment or both.

The Ford Foundation decided to send six assembly line workers from Detroit to get their reaction to the team operation. They stayed only six weeks, which in a strange country with a strange language may hardly have been long enough to form a judgment. In any event, with one exception the six said they preferred the assembly line at Cadillac to the Swedish system. Partly this had to do with local union independence as against the umbrella of the Labor Organisationen. It may have been a question of individualism as against careful organization from top to bottom, which says a lot about the United States and Sweden. It is hard for me to imagine an American motor manufacturer innovative or imaginative enough to undertake a Kalmar.

The original way in which the Swedes have attempted to cope with the helplessness of the individual in the face of government bureaucracy has contributed a word to the English language. That word is *ombudsman*. From the literal meaning of *representative* it has come to designate a preceptor, an individual given the authority to publicize and protest against abuses. The office originated in Sweden in 1809 with the establishment of a parliamentary ombudsman empowered to hear citizens' complaints and act as an independent arbiter between the government and the individual. The parliamentary ombudsman is a state official elected by parliament. He can investigate all public agencies and public officials, including courts, judges, and prosecutors. With such a broad assignment, the parliamentary ombudsman and his staff work under great pressure. The office has won public esteem as a barrier against the encroachments of big government. The success of the institution has resulted in its being used in other contexts, notably as part of the system the Swedish press has set up to monitor itself.

The initial free press law, one of the first in the West,

was adopted in 1766. The Press Council goes back to
1916. It was a voluntary organization formed by the Newspaper Publishers Association, the Union of Journalists, and the Swedish Publicists Club, an organization resembling Sigma Delta Chi, the American journalists' fraternity that now calls itself the Society of Professional Journalists. The interest of the Swedish press in creating an effective system of self-discipline derives from the extreme liberality of the free press law as contained in Sweden's constitution. Lennart Groll, the first press ombudsman for the general public, an office created in the act of 1969 (discussed below), points in an analysis of the voluntary system to the need for self-discipline, and this was particularly true at a time when the government was considering the possibility of laws putting limits on the freedom of the press.

In the late 1960s there was widespread dissatisfaction with the work of the Press Council. It was felt, according to Groll, that journalistic abuses were increasing, and they were not being brought to the attention of the Press Council. Out of this discontent came a series of reforms that went into effect in 1969. There are currently six members and several deputies, who can take part in meetings but are allowed to vote only when a member is not present. The chairman is an active or retired judge, the former president of the Swedish Supreme Court, Sven Romanus, at the time Groll was writing. Three members are nominated by the press organizations. Under the 1969 reforms, two new members were added to represent the general public and are chosen by interest groups such as the LO and SAF. The duty of promoting the freedom of the press has been assigned not to the Press Council but to a separate organization, the Cooperation Council of the Swedish Press. Made up of representatives of the press organizations, it is concerned with proposed press legislation and all matters that might impinge on fundamental freedoms.

Thus the Press Council has a clear field to consider

abuses and see that they are rectified. A newspaper that has been censured by the council is expected to publish the findings of the council and almost invariably does. Under the 1969 reforms the council is authorized to impose a fine on an offending newspaper of up to $1,200 for a paper with a circulation over 10,000. A person who has been victimized in the press cannot collect damages through the Press Council, but there is no obstacle to a simultaneous or subsequent action in a court of law.

All complaints against newspapers and magazines now go to the press ombudsman. If he thinks the complaint is well founded he refers the case to the Press Council together with the comments of the editor and his own opinion. Complaints may be rejected as not sufficiently well founded, whereupon the individual may take his case directly to the council provided he is personally affected by the article in question.

The base for the work of the council and the ombudsman is a Code of Ethics adopted by the Publicists Club in 1923. Frequently amended, in 1974 the code was augmented by a set of Ethical Rules, issued jointly by the Newspaper Publishers Association, the Union of Journalists, and the Swedish Publicists Club, which is applicable to press, radio, and television. The code and the rules stress the importance of respect for the private life of the individual. "Publicity which may constitute an invasion of privacy should be avoided short of overriding grounds for publication in the public interest." Strong restrictions are placed on the reporting of trials and police investigations. Without an overriding public interest, the names of suspected or convicted individuals are not to be reported nor, when the name of a person is not given, is the person in question to be identified by other information, such as age and occupation. Sensational fringe publications, often bordering on the pornographic, were one target of the augmented rules.

The number of complaints rose sharply when the

office of press ombudsman was instituted. About 400 complaints have been filed annually in recent years as compared with 50 before the reform. Around 20 complaints have been initiated each year by the ombudsman, mainly concerning sensational reporting of crimes and court trials. The press ombudsman, it should be stressed, has no status in law, in contrast to the parliamentary ombudsman.

One aspect of the relationship between government and the press is difficult for Americans to understand. As costs of publication rose and reputable newspapers began to have financial trouble, the government concluded it was important to prevent varying political voices from being submerged. The result was subsidies with no strings attached to bolster hard-pressed newspapers.

The subsidies are granted to "serious" newspapers, that is, in the Swedish judgment, morning newspapers, as against afternoon newspapers, which are considered entertainment. A committee of the parliament passes on the allocations by a complicated formula covering production and distribution costs and other lesser liabilities. The annual total is about $40 million, of which metropolitan newspapers get about one-third and provincial papers another third, with the balance going to weeklies and other small publications. *Svenska Dagbladet*, the principal conservative newspaper in Stockholm, currently gets a subsidy of close to $5 million.

Those in government long familiar with the system of subsidization of the press insist that it has no relation to editorial opinion. *Svenska Dagbladet* is reportedly moving up in revenue as against *Dagens Nyheter*, the nation's largest paper, which receives no subsidy. A sufficient improvement would mean an end to *Dagbladet*'s subsidy. The percentages work out to 60 percent for Socialist party newspapers, 15 percent for those voicing the Moderate or Conservative party line, 15 percent for the Center party, 5 percent for Liberal party papers, and 5 percent for those

with no party connection. As in most of Europe, newspapers in Sweden have a closer party affiliation than do newspapers in the United States and express party viewpoints.

*   *   *

The wide variety of public and private programs and activities treated in this chapter are all a reflection of the middle way—a conviction that reason can prevail in righting the wrongs of a troubled world. They represent a serious, determined effort to cope with specific problems. In each instance the citizenry have been involved either directly or indirectly. This may be the distinguishing mark of democracy in Sweden: concern, public interest, public discussion, which means participation. That 95 percent of eligible voters cast their ballots in the national election of 1976 was evidence of interest in the issues that were so hotly debated in the campaign.

Certain of the programs mean sizable government expenditure. That is true notably of the reform of the penal system that has made Sweden the conspicuous example of humane and intelligent treatment of those who violate the law. The costs of Sweden's lifestyle must come from a government with a sound financial base. And that is Sweden's dilemma today.

As we will see in chapter 3, these costs, added to the staggering cost of the wide range of benefits in the Swedish welfare state, have created new stresses and strains in the society and raised questions about the future of the middle way.

3 *Stresses and Strains*

Immediately after World War II, the Social Democrats had considered a radical departure from the moderate welfare socialism of the prewar years. Fearing a depression like that which set in after 1918, they were concerned that the Communists had made a gain of 2.4 percent in the communal elections of 1942. In the opinion of many, the party had to offer a stronger socialist line asserting the right of government to direct private production for egalitarian ends. Left-wingers in the party were contemptuous in the mid-forties of what they said was merely a social insurance system that left a few wealthy families in control of industry and business. The upshot of this thinking was the formation in 1946 of a committee made up of trade union and Social Democratic representatives.

The chairman was Ernst Wigforss, who had by then become one of the most outspoken intellectual radicals in the party. The executive director was Gunnar Myrdal. The committee formulated a 27-point program which, while it did not follow orthodox Marxist tenets, went a considerable way in the direction of nationalization of basic industries and credit institutions such as banks and insurance companies. The opening paragraph of the committee report stated:

The goal of social democracy is to reformulate the economic organization of bourgeois society so that the

right to determine production is placed in the hands of all citizens; so that the majority is freed from its dependence on a minority of capitalists; and so that a social order built on economic classes gives way to a community of free and equal citizens.

The 27-point program touched off an intense debate that transcended party lines. This seemed to be a turning point for the Socialists. Would they follow the lead of those like Wigforss who were insisting that production for use by the state must replace private enterprise? Or would they go on with the partnership between labor and industry that had prevailed through the late thirties?

The debate soon seemed to be rendered academic, however, by a swift rise in prosperity, as Sweden with its high technology and its industry more or less intact, undamaged by war, took hold in export markets with substantially increased profits. As we shall see, there were some in LO who continued during the boom years of the 1950s and 1960s to push for greater control over profits and production, but for all practical purposes a national decision had been made in favor of further development of the welfare state along lines that had become familiar. The impression still prevailed in the mid-sixties that a healthy balance had been struck between the two main elements in the economic process—industry and labor. There seemed no reason prosperity could not continue into the indefinite future. It was perhaps with the illusion that this prosperity would be sustained that the Social Democratic government, with little or no opposition from the right-of-center parties, adopted a series of welfare measures that, together with rising taxes, sharply increased the cost of industrial production and put a heavy burden on taxpayers in the middle-income brackets.

A 64-page pamphlet published under the joint auspices of the employer and employee confederations lists the measures of cradle-to-grave security in concise form, with

the agency supplying the benefits. It begins with a general family allowance for children under sixteen years of age, who receive $400 a year not subject to income tax. The child receives free health supervision up to school age from child welfare centers; this is provided by the school medical officer during term time. Dental care for children is provided by the same centers or by national dental service clinics. Inoculations and what the pamphlet calls "prophylactic medicines," vitamins, iron, etc. are provided free. Free consultation on the upbringing of children is provided by the Advice Bureau for Child and Youth Mental Care. All these services are given regardless of the family income. Fees for day nurseries for children from six months to seven years for parents who are both working or studying are adjusted to the income of the parents.

children's services

Again regardless of income, education is free at comprehensive schools, high schools, and county colleges, and advanced tuition at universities and colleges is also free, as are graduate studies. Meals are free in comprehensive and high schools, as are school books and school supplies. After the age of sixteen a student is eligible for an allowance of $30 a month. Four additional pages in the booklet are devoted to educational assistance in the form of loans and grants.

education—free

Marriage and maternity benefits range from home furnishing loans to free advice on contraception and abortion at maternity centers and hospitals and by district medical officers. A cash maternity allowance paid regardless of income is as follows:

marriage & maternity benefits

On the birth of a child a [taxable] parenthood benefit is paid to one of the parents. Prior to the birth, only the mother is entitled to parenthood benefit which becomes payable from the 60th day before the expected date of birth. After the birth of the child the benefit is paid to the parent who cares for the child. Even if the mother does not have the child in her care, she is entitled to parenthood

benefit up to and including the 29th day after the birth.
Thereafter the parents may take turns caring for the child
(even for half a day each at a time). The minimum parenthood benefit is $5 a day paid for a maximum of 210 days
per birth "regardless of how it is divided between the parents."

Foster and adoptive parents are eligible for parenthood benefits on essentially the same terms as natural parents. Services of a trained midwife are free before, during,
and after childbirth, as is the cost of confinement in a maternity hospital, the latter to include travel if a hospital is
not available in the mother's immediate neighborhood.
Beginning in 1977 sickness entitlements related to maternity were abolished and replaced by parenthood benefits
for either father or mother, the amount being equal to "the
parent's normal sickness benefit." Matrimonial problems
may be taken up at family guidance centers.

State loans for apartments and dwellings are covered
by a complex series of regulations, as are also state rent al-
lowances payable to families with at least one child under
seventeen years of age wholly or partly maintained by the
family at home. Rent allowance is available to single persons and couples without children, under elaborate formu-
las, from the central government and the municipality. The
amount of allowance per month, ranging from about $100
to $200, is based on income assessed for state income tax
and the number of children in the family.

"Social home help" is given to aged and handicapped
persons on the basis of fees in accordance with the ability
to pay; it is free to those with limited means. Holidays for
housewives are provided at reduced cost. This is made possible by grants for the running of holiday homes and for
traveling expenses to and from the holiday home or resort.
Thanks to the grants-in-aid to organizers of holiday homes,
board and lodging are kept relatively low. A flat sum is
made available for travel to the holiday home "which is

considered to provide her with the best chance for rest and recreation."

Twenty-three pages are taken up with details of the benefits under the national health insurance program and the special dispensation for industrial accidents and disablement. Sweden has perhaps the most comprehensive health insurance plan in the world. The Regional Social Insurance Office pays the costs of hospitalization at virtually all general hospitals as well as mental hospitals, tuberculosis sanitariums, cottage hospitals, homes for tractable mental patients, and Social Insurance Board hospitals for rheumatic and other diseases. Beginning in 1974 a National Dental Insurance Scheme provided a substantial reduction in the cost of dental care, with some types of treatment free. Certain vitally important medicines such as insulin are provided free, and for other medicines ordered by a doctor or dentist there is a discount of 50 percent on any cost exceeding $1. Both venereal disease patients and alcoholics receive free treatment, the latter in government hospitals where they can live under supervision and pursue their usual employment.

Beginning with the National Pension Scheme adopted by the Riksdag in its present form in 1958 and 1959 Sweden has probably the most generous of all pensions for a broad range of retired persons, the disabled, and those who are too ill to work. The basic pension was substantially increased by a series of acts providing supplements, which were increased by parliamentary action in 1974 at the same time that the basic pension was increased and the general retirement age lowered to sixty-five from sixty-seven. The employer pays a contribution, determined by an elaborate formula, on the wages of his employees; no contribution is required from the employee. A salaried person with an income of $7,000 in 1975 would get a pension of $5,200. A salary of $14,000 would bring a pension of $11,700, the maximum. The pension is adjusted to rising or falling prices.

The bill for employers for this wide range of social services is roughly 40 percent of the cost of wages. These charges—44 percent for white-collar workers—are deductible from corporate income tax.

As welfare benefits increased, along with government subsidies for surplus production, resentment became widespread among the middle and upper middle classes feeling the pinch of high taxes and ever increasing prices. A new vacation act that took effect in 1978 guaranteed a minimum of five weeks of paid vacation as against four under the previous law. Resented, too, was the reduction from three days to one day in the requirement for reporting illness before obtaining sick leave.

But the persistent theme was taxes, a theme on which the Employers Confederation kept up a constant fire. It put out figures in late 1975 showing that a male industrial worker receiving $1,900 in wages in 1950, including compulsory employer contributions, paid a total tax of $270 or 17 percent of his income. In 1975 a wage earner making an annual return of $11,200 paid a total tax of $6,800 or 60 percent of his income. Thus, as SAF pointed out, the total level of taxation for an average wage earner had more than tripled.

By comparison, a university lecturer, married with two children, in the highest salary grade, received in 1970 an annual income of $13,000, which included a child allowance of $360. His tax was $7,750. In 1975 he earned $16,200, and his net disposable income was $9,000. Taking into account the rise in prices, in 1970 money values the lecturer was receiving $6,000 in disposable income even though his overall income rose during the five-year period by 29 percent. "There was nothing left over for increased consumption," SAF observed. Instead, his standard of living fell by 22 percent. To have maintained his previous standard he would have had to have an increase in salary of $10,000. The confederation noted, too, that the difference after taxes between the wages of an industrial

worker and the salary of a lecturer had narrowed in the five-year period from 70 percent to 27 percent.

Stress in Sweden is put on what are called marginal tax rates, that is, a tax on the top 10 percent of additional income above the normal salary range. The marginal tax rate for a married worker with two children was 62 percent in 1975. As shown in a table of comparison it was the highest in the world and compared with 34 percent in Britain, 54 percent in Norway, 27 percent in Canada, and 14 percent in France. In the upper brackets the marginal tax could take 75 to 80 percent. An economics professor doing consulting work overseas told me that out of a fee of $9,000 he would have perhaps $1,000 left after the marginal levy. I spoke of the effect of this tax to a well-informed Swedish official, suggesting it was hardly an incentive for greater effort, whatever the field. His response was interesting: that is not necessarily true, he said, as money rewards are not so important as titles—engineer, professor, whatever; this you will see by glancing at any telephone book.

In 1973 and 1974 Swedish industrial firms made large profits. This was quickly translated by the Labor Organisationen into "excess profits," with demands for wage increases exceeding anything in the past. At the same time the cost in industrial production of new welfare reforms was added on to the production bill. For example, the reduction in the requirement to report illness before obtaining sick leave resulted in a rate of absenteeism as high, if not higher, than any in the industrialized world. Wildcat strikes occurred with a frequency hitherto unknown. The phenomenon called in Sweden "wage drift" further enhanced the upward movement of wages. The stability of the past, under the pact of Saltsjobaden, was badly shattered.

Against this background Sweden was confronted with a worldwide recession, the most serious since that of the thirties, and with the quadrupling of oil prices following the embargo in the aftermath of the 1973 Arab-Israeli war.

oil price +
trade deficit

Sweden is nearly as dependent on imports for energy, both oil and coal, as Japan. And even though, as we have seen, energy consumption is proportionately 37 percent less than that in the United States, oil imports quickly contributed to a growing trade deficit. It was small consolation that neighboring Norway had struck an oil bonanza in the North Sea. A similar prize had escaped the Swedes despite repeated explorations.

A conscientious, order-keeping people, the Swedes give off charts and statistics in profusion. After 1974 it was evident that with the necessity to export up to 50 percent of industrial production the economy was in serious trouble. As one chart after another showed, the nation was living beyond its means, with fixed charges in wages and welfare costs exceeding those in every other industrialized country.

In 1975 the average total cost per hour for adult male workers was $8.50. This was the highest for any European nation, with Norway and Denmark close runners up. The hourly rate for Japan was roughly half that for Sweden. The average figure for the United States was approximately $7 in 1976 currency. Wage costs had gone up roughly 45 percent in little more than two years. Faced with the charge of excess profits and fearful of a general strike that would over a period of many weeks put an end to all profits, the leading industrialists had capitulated to the demands for wage increases. Wage costs in the Federal Republic of Germany, perhaps Sweden's principal customer, had advanced only 11 percent. It was an intolerable situation and no one, whether of the right or the left, seemed to have any immediate solution.

Certain events were occurring that threw this painful dilemma into sharp perspective, with repercussions both at home and abroad. One was the angry outburst of Ingmar Bergman when he was charged with income tax evasion and taken from a rehearsal at the Dramatic Theater before a tax court.

Ingmar
Bergman
case

Bergman went to Munich, where his first undertaking was a production of the Strindberg play. He then began work on a film with Liv Ullman and David Carradine as the principals, playing two down-at-heel circus performers trying to make a living in Germany in the early twenties as the Nazis began their rise to power. Called *The Serpent's Egg* it was unlike Bergman's other work in that it was charged with political prophecies anticipating the rise of Hitler and with a crude violence such as he had never employed before. When it was shown abroad critics were harsh. They suggested that if this was the consequence of his transplantation he should return to Sweden.

Not long after the Bergman case there was another attack on the Swedish tax system. It came from Astrid Lindgren, a well-known author of children's stories that have been translated into many languages around the world. She wrote an article for the newspaper *Expressen* putting in the concept of a fantasy that she would have to pay more than her entire income for 1976 in taxes. Not as famous as Bergman, she nevertheless had a wide following and she had long been a member of the Social Democratic party, although now with the tax what it was she said she had become skeptical. Her article attracted wide attention in radio and television, and it was the subject of a debate in the Riksdag.

It developed that the 100 percent levy on Lindgren's income grew out of a section of the tax law imposing on employers "social charges," in effect a tax on wages that covers pensions and social insurance for employees. This amounted to about 40 percent of an employee's wages. Persons practising a "free profession," that is, lawyers, private doctors, dentists, artists, and authors, had to pay their own social charges.

In the spring of 1975 the Social Democrats, the Center party, and the Liberals held a conference on taxation in which they agreed on certain changes in the law that were supposed to eliminate the possibility that professionals in a

Bergman had a unique place in his own country and the world. In the art of film he was an heir to Ibsen and Strindberg, the dramatists of Norway and Sweden, whose plays explored the deep vein of gloom in the Scandinavian temperament. They confronted the bland surface of bourgeois life with bitter truths, as in Ibsen's social dramas such as *An Enemy of the People* and *Ghosts*. One of Strindberg's early works, *The Red Room*, was a satirical account of the abuses and wrongs of Stockholm society. Both dramatists won wide audiences, and often hostile criticism, around the world and set the tone for much that followed.

In the same way Bergman's films have won acceptance far beyond the borders of his native land. He has been more interested in exploring the profound sorrow of man's fate faced with the inevitability of mortality rather than the social ills of the time. One of his latest films, *Cries and Whispers*, about a woman dying of cancer and the ordeal of her family, is almost intolerable in its sorrow and misery. Earlier pictures such as *Wild Strawberries* are not quite so harsh, yet they convey the same sense of man's doom. A version of his *Smiles of a Summer Night*, called on Broadway *A Little Night Music*, was lightened by charming thematic music and excellent acting, much of it striking a humorous note. Yet it, too, had an underlying theme of man's contradictory role in seeking happiness while facing his inevitable end.

If the Swedish tax assessors had deliberately set out to dramatize on a world stage the severity of the tax system they could hardly have succeeded more admirably than in the Bergman case. Temperamental, high-strung, Bergman was nevertheless capable of intense concentration both in the theater and in films. He had been married five times and had had a long liaison with Liv Ullman, the actress whom he had helped to make a star. She bore him a daughter. After a hectic, hard-driven life for nine or ten months of the year he retreated to the island of Fårön in the Baltic, where in a summer house he treasured his privacy and the

calm of the sea and the shore.

The background of the Bergman case was as follows. Toward the end of the sixties he had planned a center for the production of international films. For this purpose he established a company, Persona Films AG, in Switzerland. The plan for production was, however, abandoned. Persona was instead used to collect income from Bergman films played abroad. When the Riksbank, the Swedish Central Bank, pointed out that Persona was not being used for film production, the company was shut down and its assets amounting to about $600,000 were sent to Sweden. The suspicions of the tax collectors were aroused by the fact that the company had been established in Switzerland. A great deal of controversy has centered on charges that business firms have sought to take advantage of low Swiss taxes as against Sweden's high taxes.

Following a survey of Bergman's extensive tax returns, the assessor ruled that Persona Films AG was established only to evade Swedish fiscal legislation. This meant that the $600,000 was in fact a concealed salary, and Bergman must pay a tax on the cumulative amounts for the years 1969-74. The tax under the ruling covered virtually the entire amount. The assessor sent the case against Bergman and his lawyer, who had helped to set up Persona, to the prosecutor. The wheels began to turn irrevocably, with consequences that apparently no one in high office had foreseen.

The rehearsal of Strindberg's *Dance of Death* at the Dramatic Theater was interrupted by the tax police, who came to bring Bergman to a court of inquiry. Several actors from the company went with Bergman to the scene of the inquiry. The prosecutor's justification for such hasty and arbitrary action was that it was necessary in order to prevent the film director from escaping abroad. With the outraged director and his players it might have been out of one of Bergman's own pictures. At the same time the prosecution had searched both Bergman's house and that of his

lawyer, and documents had been confiscated. In early February 1976 Bergman was prosecuted for tax evasion and "careless income tax returns."

A loud outcry with national and international publicity followed the episode at the Dramatic Theater. In the indignant reaction both in the press and in public opinion the tax assessors were accused of seeking publicity by bringing a charge against so prominent an individual. The case was said to be weak, hardly justifying such arbitrary action. It was persecution of an artist, commentators said, and this was the reaction abroad. The Bergman case was widely debated on radio and television. Only *Aftonbladet*, the Stockholm daily owned by the Labor Organisationer came to the defense of the tax assessors. It was hypocris to weep over Bergman's plight, the paper argued, sin many others suspected of evading tax laws had receiv the same treatment with little or no public protest. All ci zens should be treated alike, no matter what their names positions. Tax officials were properly concerned with and all efforts to frustrate the Swedish tax system thro the Swiss route.

As the outcry continued, the chief public prose intervened and asked the county prosecutor to try case. An investigation at this level showed that the ch were not justified. In April the case was dro Realizing how harmful the publicity had been as the tion approached, Prime Minister Olof Palme telepl Bergman to express his regret at the way the case ha handled.

For the great film director all this came too few days after he was taken before the prosecutor fered a nervous collapse and was hospitalized. nounced shortly after the case was dropped that leaving Sweden to live and work abroad. He wou his disposable assets behind, so no one would thin trying to escape further claims by the tax assess was a severe blow: the loss of an artist of worl

high-income bracket—$40,000 a year or more—would
have to pay their entire income in taxes. Employers were
to be allowed a tax deduction in the same year that they
paid the social charges for their employees, but professionals were not permitted such a deduction until the following
year. In the debate that followed, the finance minister in
the Social Democratic government, Gunnar Sträng, admitted that a mistake had been made at the tax conference,
and the error was corrected, so that professionals could not
be taxed all or even more than their total annual income.

"error"

But the damage had been done, and, as a national
election in 1976 approached, few doubted that this drama-
tization of the welfare and high wage system had harmed
the Social Democrats, in power for nearly forty-four years.
At the same time, the rapid rise in prices reached phenom-
enal levels. Housewives were indignant at what they had to
pay at the check-out counter. The official rate of inflation
climbed to 13 percent. The "value-added" tax on everything, including many medicines and food, was due to go
from 10 to 20 percent.*

As complaints about high taxes and high prices grew,
so did the means of avoiding these taxes. Thus an auto me-
chanic would perform services for the owner of a clothing
store in return for a winter coat, with no money changing
hands. One estimate put the extent of this form of barter at
7 percent of the total of individual taxes due the state.

barter grew

Another source of dissatisfaction with the Social
Democratic government related to day care centers. With
70 percent of women between the ages of twenty and
sixty-four employed, the government was pushing a
greatly expanded program of day care centers. Working
mothers complained that the number of such centers was
woefully inadequate and because of their uneven distribution in the cities children had to be transported in the early
morning for an hour or more to the nearest center.

probs. with
day care
centers

* The value-added tax, in wide use in Europe, is a multistage sales tax
based on the net value added to a taxable product by a firm.

*another prob.
for S. Dem. Party
the
Meidner
plan*

It was, however, a political issue with echoes out of the past that probably did more to hurt the Social Democrats in the 1976 election than high prices and high taxes and inadequate day care centers. And the central figure could hardly have been in greater contrast to Bergman with his dramatic flair and his worldwide reputation. Rudolph Meidner had come to Stockholm as a refugee from Nazi Germany. An economist with a thorough grounding in the social sciences and economics, he was modest, self-effacing, even shy. Meidner quickly found a place among the intellectuals and ideologues of the trade union movement and the Social Democratic party. While his grasp of the economics of his adopted land, from the perspective of the trade union movement, was unquestioned, the repercussions which came out of what was to be known as the Meidner plan could hardly have been anticipated.

For thirty years he was the chief economist of the Labor Organisationen. In that capacity he helped to promote the policy of trade union solidarity, that is, an equalization of the rate of pay as between low-paid and high-paid workers. That has been the core of Swedish trade union ideology, pushed so tenaciously that today the difference between the two extremes is scarcely more than 10 percent. But it did not answer the question of the relationship among profits, the narrow control over private industrial production, and the broad mass of a labor force more than 95 percent unionized whether in LO or in the white-collar unions.

Meidner went through the post-1945 crisis when high unemployment was expected as had occurred after the First World War. The Wigforss commission, with Gunnar Myrdal as executive director, came up with its 27-point program, most of the points written by Meidner's associate Gösta Rehn, proposing nationalization of the banks and insurance companies. It was a radical program anticipating trade union power when, in a period of mass unem-

ployment, the public would be in a mood to accept it. But with high employment in a booming economy the unions lost interest in the report. Meidner continued to believe that the trade union movement must face up to control of profits.

In 1961 Meidner helped to draft an LO report that proposed building up the funds of branch unions and negotiating with industry on "excess" profits. It called for joint union and industry administration of research and education. Meidner believed this was considerably in advance of the German trade union plan, which had its base in profit sharing by individual workers. Three of Sweden's largest unions rejected the plan and so did LO at its annual meeting that year. Particularly frustrating for Meidner was that there had been no discussion of the proposal in the newspapers. Five years later he directed preparation of an LO report under the title *Trade Unions and Technological Change*. Again this evoked no discussion.

Feeling that his efforts had been futile, Meidner accepted an offer from the government to head a new institute for research into the labor market. But he soon discovered that there were insufficient resources to conduct any meaningful research. At this point he had a long discussion with Arne Geijer, who for many years had been head of LO. Widely respected for his skill as a negotiator, Geijer had presided during the years of high prosperity when the pact of Saltsjobaden still had validity. But conditions had changed, and Geijer had concluded that something had to be done.

The number of wildcat strikes had greatly increased, reflecting LO's lack of control. A strong incentive for labor action was the belief that the tax system was tilted in favor of industry. Sizable tax reductions were granted to business for capital reinvestment, and with the boom most firms were able to use company capital for expansion. According to one estimate $7.5 billion was available for later reinvestment thanks to the tax laws. Young ideologues in

the unions had also stressed the power of multinational companies, more based in Sweden than any other country, a trend that had begun thirty years before. Two of the largest, L. M. Eriksson and SKF, had 10 percent of their labor force in Sweden and 90 percent outside the country. Another factor was the report of a royal commission of inquiry on the living standards of 6,500 individuals, which showed startlingly low levels for a high percentage of those surveyed. Almost one-third of the nation's working population lived at or below a relative standard of poverty. A shocking aspect was the way in which disabled persons were being thrown out of the labor force and then were queuing up for jobs of any sort.

Something, Geijer said, had to be done. Meidner was persuaded to return to LO. Geijer commissioned him to make proposals to the 1976 convention of LO on a number of aspects of the economy, especially to counteract the concentration of wealth by means of co-ownership through some kind of fund and co-influence in the decision-making process. It was a large order. In collaboration with younger economists in LO Meidner set out to fulfill it. The unions were not interested in individual profit-sharing plans, and on the basis of his own experience Meidner had ruled it out at the beginning. He had served on the board of directors of one of the nation's leading banks, and that bank had been able to put through a satisfactory profit-sharing plan. But the savings banks, with at least as many employees, were unable to adopt such a plan, and this had caused bad feeling.

So here was a challenge invoking the fundamental beliefs of many unionists and particularly the leaders of the metal workers, the largest and most influential union. The question was essentially this: Is it possible to achieve socialism by peaceful democratic means? Where does the control over major decisions that shape the economy really lie? In Sweden, Meidner believed, 100 individuals made the decisions: the executives and major stockholders of the

principal concerns. It is a question that troubles not only Sweden but the entire industrial West. In Britain the trade unions have pressed consistently for more and more government ownership. In the United States, publication of *Politics and Markets*, by Professor Charles E. Lindblom of Yale University, developing the thesis that the power of government cannot rival the decisive power of the great corporations, was sufficient to touch off an angry blast from the defenders of free enterprise. Even mention of the power of private industry has been deeply disturbing, although no element, certainly not the trade union movement in America, has suggested anything like the proposal that was to come before the LO convention of 1976.

The Meidner plan provided that an estimated 20 percent of the profits of companies with a fixed number of employees—whether 50 or 100 was the subject of debate—should go annually into a fund to be administered, under a complex structure, by an overall union board and by unions in particular industries:

the plan

Its purpose would be to administer the capital of the fund and to disburse that part of the yield or income of the fund which did not have to be pre-empted for the purchase by the fund of any new share issues made by companies; this remaining income would be used to promote trade union activities among all the members, with priority being given to employees in small firms. Other possible uses of the income would be for trade union education and training, safety at work, research and cultural and recreational facilities.

Throughout, it was stressed that this was to be a common endeavor with no individual reward that would increase the rate of domestic consumption if it were paid out to individuals on a profit-sharing basis. Meidner had long been convinced that profit sharing on the German plan, with the shares of the individual worker subsidized by the

government, was opposed by most employees and further-more was very costly.

Up to 100,000 union members took part in discussions before the LO convention met. A great deal of past history was rehearsed. Wage solidarity was all very well, and certainly LO was of the firm opinion that workers doing similar jobs should not find that they had markedly different pay levels because of the difference in profitability between one firm and another. But the success of the solidarity policy had depended on the willingness of high-wage groups in more profitable companies to refrain from taking full advantage of the companies' capacity to pay. This had resulted in turn in what the unions considered excess profits, which was a particularly sensitive issue in times of booming prosperity. As an LO report on the discussion preparatory to a decision said:

It is important to notice that the wages policy of solidarity and its awkward consequences for income distribution is only *one* of the factors underlying this investigation. A *second* relates to a very much more fundamental and all-embracing problem of distribution which has its roots in the fact that a significant proportion of capital growth in Sweden occurs through self-financing on the part of companies and thus accrues to the owners of capital. This problem is not new either. As a matter of fact self-financing on the part of industry, i.e. its capacity to pay for a substantial part of its capital formation out of its own profits, is a distinctive feature of our economic system. The Swedish tax system favors this self-financing through various concessions which it allows for retained savings which are used to finance new investment.

Given "some degree of self-financing," the basic question raised in the debate was whether the entire increase in the assets of the private companies should accrue to the existing "owners of capital." The dilemma had become increasingly acute between the cry for more invest-

principal concerns. It is a question that troubles not only Sweden but the entire industrial West. In Britain the trade unions have pressed consistently for more and more government ownership. In the United States, publication of *Politics and Markets*, by Professor Charles E. Lindblom of Yale University, developing the thesis that the power of government cannot rival the decisive power of the great corporations, was sufficient to touch off an angry blast from the defenders of free enterprise. Even mention of the power of private industry has been deeply disturbing, although no element, certainly not the trade union movement in America, has suggested anything like the proposal that was to come before the LO convention of 1976.

The Meidner plan provided that an estimated 20 percent of the profits of companies with a fixed number of employees—whether 50 or 100 was the subject of debate—should go annually into a fund to be administered, under a complex structure, by an overall union board and by unions in particular industries:

the plan

Its purpose would be to administer the capital of the fund and to disburse that part of the yield or income of the fund which did not have to be pre-empted for the purchase by the fund of any new share issues made by companies; this remaining income would be used to promote trade union activities among all the members, with priority being given to employees in small firms. Other possible uses of the income would be for trade union education and training, safety at work, research and cultural and recreational facilities.

Throughout, it was stressed that this was to be a common endeavor with no individual reward that would increase the rate of domestic consumption if it were paid out to individuals on a profit-sharing basis. Meidner had long been convinced that profit sharing on the German plan, with the shares of the individual worker subsidized by the

the unions had also stressed the power of multinational companies, more based in Sweden than any other country, a trend that had begun thirty years before. Two of the largest, L. M. Eriksson and SKF, had 10 percent of their labor force in Sweden and 90 percent outside the country. Another factor was the report of a royal commission of inquiry on the living standards of 6,500 individuals, which showed startlingly low levels for a high percentage of those surveyed. Almost one-third of the nation's working population lived at or below a relative standard of poverty. A shocking aspect was the way in which disabled persons were being thrown out of the labor force and then were queuing up for jobs of any sort.

Something, Geijer said, had to be done. Meidner was persuaded to return to LO. Geijer commissioned him to make proposals to the 1976 convention of LO on a number of aspects of the economy, especially to counteract the concentration of wealth by means of co-ownership through some kind of fund and co-influence in the decision-making process. It was a large order. In collaboration with younger economists in LO Meidner set out to fulfill it. The unions were not interested in individual profit-sharing plans, and on the basis of his own experience Meidner had ruled it out at the beginning. He had served on the board of directors of one of the nation's leading banks, and that bank had been able to put through a satisfactory profit-sharing plan. But the savings banks, with at least as many employees, were unable to adopt such a plan, and this had caused bad feeling.

So here was a challenge invoking the fundamental beliefs of many unionists and particularly the leaders of the metal workers, the largest and most influential union. The question was essentially this: Is it possible to achieve socialism by peaceful democratic means? Where does the control over major decisions that shape the economy really lie? In Sweden, Meidner believed, 100 individuals made the decisions: the executives and major stockholders of the

ployment, the public would be in a mood to accept it. But
with high employment in a booming economy the unions lost interest in the report. Meidner continued to believe that the trade union movement must face up to control of profits.

In 1961 Meidner helped to draft an LO report that proposed building up the funds of branch unions and negotiating with industry on "excess" profits. It called for joint union and industry administration of research and education. Meidner believed this was considerably in advance of the German trade union plan, which had its base in profit sharing by individual workers. Three of Sweden's largest unions rejected the plan and so did LO at its annual meeting that year. Particularly frustrating for Meidner was that there had been no discussion of the proposal in the newspapers. Five years later he directed preparation of an LO report under the title *Trade Unions and Technological Change*. Again this evoked no discussion.

Feeling that his efforts had been futile, Meidner accepted an offer from the government to head a new institute for research into the labor market. But he soon discovered that there were insufficient resources to conduct any meaningful research. At this point he had a long discussion with Arne Geijer, who for many years had been head of LO. Widely respected for his skill as a negotiator, Geijer had presided during the years of high prosperity when the pact of Saltsjobaden still had validity. But conditions had changed, and Geijer had concluded that something had to be done.

The number of wildcat strikes had greatly increased, reflecting LO's lack of control. A strong incentive for labor action was the belief that the tax system was tilted in favor of industry. Sizable tax reductions were granted to business for capital reinvestment, and with the boom most firms were able to use company capital for expansion. According to one estimate $7.5 billion was available for later reinvestment thanks to the tax laws. Young ideologues in

another prob.
for S. Dem. Party

the
Meidner
plan

It was, however, a political issue with echoes out of the past that probably did more to hurt the Social Democrats in the 1976 election than high prices and high taxes and inadequate day care centers. And the central figure could hardly have been in greater contrast to Bergman with his dramatic flair and his worldwide reputation. Rudolph Meidner had come to Stockholm as a refugee from Nazi Germany. An economist with a thorough grounding in the social sciences and economics, he was modest, self-effacing, even shy. Meidner quickly found a place among the intellectuals and ideologues of the trade union movement and the Social Democratic party. While his grasp of the economics of his adopted land, from the perspective of the trade union movement, was unquestioned, the repercussions which came out of what was to be known as the Meidner plan could hardly have been anticipated.

For thirty years he was the chief economist of the Labor Organisationen. In that capacity he helped to promote the policy of trade union solidarity, that is, an equalization of the rate of pay as between low-paid and high-paid workers. That has been the core of Swedish trade union ideology, pushed so tenaciously that today the difference between the two extremes is scarcely more than 10 percent. But it did not answer the question of the relationship among profits, the narrow control over private industrial production, and the broad mass of a labor force more than 95 percent unionized whether in LO or in the white-collar unions.

Meidner went through the post-1945 crisis when high unemployment was expected as had occurred after the First World War. The Wigforss commission, with Gunnar Myrdal as executive director, came up with its 27-point program, most of the points written by Meidner's associate Gösta Rehn, proposing nationalization of the banks and insurance companies. It was a radical program anticipating trade union power when, in a period of mass unem-

high-income bracket—$40,000 a year or more—would
have to pay their entire income in taxes. Employers were
to be allowed a tax deduction in the same year that they
paid the social charges for their employees, but professionals were not permitted such a deduction until the following
year. In the debate that followed, the finance minister in
the Social Democratic government, Gunnar Sträng, admitted that a mistake had been made at the tax conference,
and the error was corrected, so that professionals could not
be taxed all or even more than their total annual income.

But the damage had been done, and, as a national
election in 1976 approached, few doubted that this drama-
tization of the welfare and high wage system had harmed
the Social Democrats, in power for nearly forty-four years.
At the same time, the rapid rise in prices reached phenom-
enal levels. Housewives were indignant at what they had to
pay at the check-out counter. The official rate of inflation
climbed to 13 percent. The "value-added" tax on everything, including many medicines and food, was due to go
from 10 to 20 percent.*

As complaints about high taxes and high prices grew,
so did the means of avoiding these taxes. Thus an auto me-
chanic would perform services for the owner of a clothing
store in return for a winter coat, with no money changing
hands. One estimate put the extent of this form of barter at
7 percent of the total of individual taxes due the state.

Another source of dissatisfaction with the Social
Democratic government related to day care centers. With
70 percent of women between the ages of twenty and
sixty-four employed, the government was pushing a
greatly expanded program of day care centers. Working
mothers complained that the number of such centers was
woefully inadequate and because of their uneven distribution in the cities children had to be transported in the early
morning for an hour or more to the nearest center.

* The value-added tax, in wide use in Europe, is a multistage sales tax
based on the net value added to a taxable product by a firm.

lawyer, and documents had been confiscated. In early February 1976 Bergman was prosecuted for tax evasion and "careless income tax returns."

A loud outcry with national and international publicity followed the episode at the Dramatic Theater. In the indignant reaction both in the press and in public opinion the tax assessors were accused of seeking publicity by bringing a charge against so prominent an individual. The case was said to be weak, hardly justifying such arbitrary action. It was persecution of an artist, commentators said, and this was the reaction abroad. The Bergman case was widely debated on radio and television. Only *Aftonbladet*, the Stockholm daily owned by the Labor Organisationen, came to the defense of the tax assessors. It was hypocrisy to weep over Bergman's plight, the paper argued, since many others suspected of evading tax laws had received the same treatment with little or no public protest. All citizens should be treated alike, no matter what their names or positions. Tax officials were properly concerned with any and all efforts to frustrate the Swedish tax system through the Swiss route.

As the outcry continued, the chief public prosecutor intervened and asked the county prosecutor to try the case. An investigation at this level showed that the charges were not justified. In April the case was dropped. Realizing how harmful the publicity had been as the election approached, Prime Minister Olof Palme telephoned Bergman to express his regret at the way the case had been handled.

For the great film director all this came too late. A few days after he was taken before the prosecutor he suffered a nervous collapse and was hospitalized. He announced shortly after the case was dropped that he was leaving Sweden to live and work abroad. He would leave his disposable assets behind, so no one would think he was trying to escape further claims by the tax assessor. Here was a severe blow: the loss of an artist of world stature.

Bergman went to Munich, where his first undertaking was
a production of the Strindberg play. He then began work
on a film with Liv Ullman and David Carradine as the
principals, playing two down-at-heel circus performers trying to make a living in Germany in the early twenties as the
Nazis began their rise to power. Called *The Serpent's Egg* it
was unlike Bergman's other work in that it was charged
with political prophecies anticipating the rise of Hitler and
with a crude violence such as he had never employed before. When it was shown abroad critics were harsh. They
suggested that if this was the consequence of his transplantation he should return to Sweden.

Not long after the Bergman case there was another
attack on the Swedish tax system. It came from Astrid
Lindgren, a well-known author of children's stories that
have been translated into many languages around the
world. She wrote an article for the newspaper *Expressen*
putting in the concept of a fantasy that she would have to
pay more than her entire income for 1976 in taxes. Not as
famous as Bergman, she nevertheless had a wide following
and she had long been a member of the Social Democratic
party, although now with the tax what it was she said she
had become skeptical. Her article attracted wide attention
in radio and television, and it was the subject of a debate in
the Riksdag.

It developed that the 100 percent levy on Lindgren's
income grew out of a section of the tax law imposing on
employers "social charges," in effect a tax on wages that
covers pensions and social insurance for employees. This
amounted to about 40 percent of an employee's wages.
Persons practising a "free profession," that is, lawyers, private doctors, dentists, artists, and authors, had to pay their
own social charges.

In the spring of 1975 the Social Democrats, the Center party, and the Liberals held a conference on taxation in
which they agreed on certain changes in the law that were
supposed to eliminate the possibility that professionals in a

calm of the sea and the shore.

The background of the Bergman case was as follows. Toward the end of the sixties he had planned a center for the production of international films. For this purpose he established a company, Persona Films AG, in Switzerland. The plan for production was, however, abandoned. Persona was instead used to collect income from Bergman films played abroad. When the Riksbank, the Swedish Central Bank, pointed out that Persona was not being used for film production, the company was shut down and its assets amounting to about $600,000 were sent to Sweden. The suspicions of the tax collectors were aroused by the fact that the company had been established in Switzerland. A great deal of controversy has centered on charges that business firms have sought to take advantage of low Swiss taxes as against Sweden's high taxes.

Following a survey of Bergman's extensive tax returns, the assessor ruled that Persona Films AG was established only to evade Swedish fiscal legislation. This meant that the $600,000 was in fact a concealed salary, and Bergman must pay a tax on the cumulative amounts for the years 1969-74. The tax under the ruling covered virtually the entire amount. The assessor sent the case against Bergman and his lawyer, who had helped to set up Persona, to the prosecutor. The wheels began to turn irrevocably, with consequences that apparently no one in high office had foreseen.

The rehearsal of Strindberg's *Dance of Death* at the Dramatic Theater was interrupted by the tax police, who came to bring Bergman to a court of inquiry. Several actors from the company went with Bergman to the scene of the inquiry. The prosecutor's justification for such hasty and arbitrary action was that it was necessary in order to prevent the film director from escaping abroad. With the outraged director and his players it might have been out of one of Bergman's own pictures. At the same time the prosecution had searched both Bergman's house and that of his

Bergman had a unique place in his own country and the world. In the art of film he was an heir to Ibsen and Strindberg, the dramatists of Norway and Sweden, whose plays explored the deep vein of gloom in the Scandinavian temperament. They confronted the bland surface of bourgeois life with bitter truths, as in Ibsen's social dramas such as *An Enemy of the People* and *Ghosts*. One of Strindberg's early works, *The Red Room*, was a satirical account of the abuses and wrongs of Stockholm society. Both dramatists won wide audiences, and often hostile criticism, around the world and set the tone for much that followed.

In the same way Bergman's films have won acceptance far beyond the borders of his native land. He has been more interested in exploring the profound sorrow of man's fate faced with the inevitability of mortality rather than the social ills of the time. One of his latest films, *Cries and Whispers*, about a woman dying of cancer and the ordeal of her family, is almost intolerable in its sorrow and misery. Earlier pictures such as *Wild Strawberries* are not quite so harsh, yet they convey the same sense of man's doom. A version of his *Smiles of a Summer Night*, called on Broadway *A Little Night Music*, was lightened by charming thematic music and excellent acting, much of it striking a humorous note. Yet it, too, had an underlying theme of man's contradictory role in seeking happiness while facing his inevitable end.

If the Swedish tax assessors had deliberately set out to dramatize on a world stage the severity of the tax system they could hardly have succeeded more admirably than in the Bergman case. Temperamental, high-strung, Bergman was nevertheless capable of intense concentration both in the theater and in films. He had been married five times and had had a long liaison with Liv Ullman, the actress whom he had helped to make a star. She bore him a daughter. After a hectic, hard-driven life for nine or ten months of the year he retreated to the island of Fårön in the Baltic, where in a summer house he treasured his privacy and the

ment on the one hand and the demand for greater justice in the structure of ownership on the other. These were men and women representatives of what is surely one of the most disciplined trade union movements in the world, discussing with the utmost seriousness a fundamental issue of the controls exercised over the economy of which they were a part. It was noted that reforms had been proposed in some countries which had stirred wide attention beyond the confines of the trade union movement. This unfortunately had not happened in Sweden.

In light of the lengthy educational drive within union locals around the country, adoption of the Meidner report was a foregone conclusion. The LO Congress expressed the decision as follows:

The Executive Board stressed that the Meidner report was setting out the basic principles plus an outline sketch of possible arrangements. The Congress accepted these guidelines as the basis on which to pursue the matter further. The Executive also indicated that it wished to keep an open stance on the various details of the possible scheme that might finally be adopted, such as the rate of buildup of the funds, the scope of the system, and the administration of the funds. A Royal Commission under the chairmanship of one of the country governors in Sweden, Mr. Mehr, has recently been appointed to look at the whole subject of "employees and the growth of company capital," and the Executive made it clear to the Congress that it expects the Royal Commission to make detailed proposals on which LO will then be able to make detailed comments which take account of the points made at the Congress.

Although this seemed to indicate that the conclusion of the royal commission might result in modification of the Meidner plan, it was plain that the all-powerful trade union organization had come out for the core of the proposal, which was that 20 percent of company profits should go into a common fund administered by the unions.

An immediate outcry went up from industry and the right-of-center parties. This was confiscation. If the Meidner plan were to be enacted by the Riskdag it would mean that within fifteen years, or perhaps even less, the unions would control all of industry, with the exception of a few smaller companies.

Overshadowing the indignation that the high tax structure had evoked, the Meidner plan was to be a central issue of the elections in September 1976. The leader of the Conservative party, Gösta Bohman, who was to be minister of the economy in the new government, called it garbage, fit only to be thrown out. With whom would the unions bargain over wages if they controlled industry? This question was repeatedly raised as the attack on the Meidner plan continued.

The concern of private industry was expressed through a variety of means, particularly through the Confederation of Employers (SAF). It was also directed at the codetermination act passed by the Riksdag in May 1976, to go into effect on January 1, 1977. Since 1974 the boards of directors of most large-scale companies had had to include representatives from the trade unions serving in their particular industry. While they were a minority, they participated in all decisions taken at the highest level on a basis of equality with the shareholders comprising the board. But the codetermination act went much further. A pamphlet put out by the Ministry of Labor specified the extent to which workers would share in the decision-making process. As interpreted by the ministry, the law seemed to preempt rights that had long been taken for granted by the employer:

The principle whereby the employer alone was entitled to organize and assign work and could freely engage and dismiss workers has been replaced by a statutory requirement that collective agreements be concluded setting out the rights of workers in respect of joint regulation.

Trade unions are henceforth entitled to resort to industrial action if such collective agreements fail to materialize; this is termed a "residual" right to industrial action.

Should a dispute arise over such matters as a worker's obligation to perform certain tasks, or the implementation of a joint regulation agreement, the trade union organization that negotiated the agreement with the employer will now enjoy a priority right of interpretation; in other words, its opinion will hold good until a settlement is reached voluntarily between the parties, or the Labor Court has ruled on the issue.

SAF was also concerned about the growing involvement of the government in the private sector through its management of pension funds. The three General Pension Funds established around 1960 manage funds of nearly $20 billion. The capacity of the funds to lend and refinance gives them a remarkable degree of power in the market. At the beginning of 1976, loans for expanding electric power amounted to almost $1 billion. Of this, roughly $300 million went into the construction of nuclear reactors, in accord with the program of the Social Democratic government, with the reactor plants as security. Loans to the town of Lulea for housing, in connection with the development of a new steel plant, made that town by far the largest borrower in 1975. The refinancing of export credits is an important function of the fund. One such project was a 35-story trade center in Warsaw. Many of the projects refinanced by the funds are built by Swedish companies.

The three funds cannot own shares of stock. But in 1974 a fourth fund was established with the sole purpose of buying and owning shares in private companies. This touched off an indignant reaction in the SAF and the nonsocialist parties. It was, they said, a disguised form of socialization. In 1976 the fourth fund was increased from $100 million to $200 million. Among its holdings the fund had about 6 percent of the capital stock of Volvo. This was

the "fourth fund": Using pension funds to purchase stocks

linked inevitably by critics on the right with the Meidner plan. It would put power over private industry in a public body that might eventually take over control from the shareholders.

As the September elections drew nearer, SAF put out a report proposing a profit-sharing plan for employees. The study, initiated in 1974, had been carried out under the direction of a committee headed by Erland Waldenstrom, the chairman of the board of Gränges, and the managing directors of other major Swedish companies, together with leading economists. The Waldenstrom report began by pointing to declining profit ratios in Swedish industry—2.2 percent in the years 1970-74; with an inflation rate of 8 percent real profits amounted to only 1.3 percent. Real profits, according to the report, had declined constantly since World War II.

With the low level of self-financing (contrary to the assumptions on which the Meidner plan was based), a way had to be found to speed up the formation of risk capital for investment in business. The answer was a system of voluntary savings by employees in the form of company shares. The annual savings proposed—1 percent of wages —would be blocked for from five to ten years. If the savings were cashed in at the end of the period, the employee would pay a tax at a reduced rate, with a lower rate for money left in for a longer period. The system would therefore be based on wages, with an added government subsidy, and the 1 percent set aside for the individual worker would not be subject to income tax. The goal was to increase savings and thereby enlarge the pool available for investment capital and expansion of industry along with an expansion in the number of jobs to be filled. The issue was thus clearly drawn between individual profit sharing and a fund controlled by the unions based on an annual assessment of company profits. In a summary, the employer's group fired a blast at LO's proposal:

The Meidner plan would result in confiscatory losses in the assets of today's shareholders, difficulties in attracting capital to companies and the eventual disappearance of the Swedish stock market. It would have very serious effects on business transactions between Sweden and other countries. Foreign companies would not wish to expand or perhaps even maintain their operations in Sweden, while Swedish companies would be increasingly inclined to move their activities overseas. The Meidner proposal would have especially serious effects on small companies which are already experiencing economic difficulties. They would gradually transform our current mixed economy into a mixed socialistic system where power over economic policy would be shared according to unclear principles between trade unions and the state. This double role for the trade unions, as representatives of both employees and owners, must seem extremely dubious even from the standpoint of the labor movement itself.

While the issue was thus sharply drawn and the right-of-center parties hammered away ceaselessly at the Meidner plan, the response of the Social Democrats was curiously ambiguous, reflecting an ambiguity within the party. Prime Minister Palme seemed to have recognized from the outset that the Meidner plan, coupled with high taxes and soaring prices, would alienate moderate and middle-of-the-road voters. Palme himself is an example of the duality of a party professedly socialist. He is from an upper-class, one might almost say aristocratic, background, and his wife is said to have a connection with royalty. Brilliant, highly articulate, he was the first Socialist prime minister to break the pattern of the past to give an intellectual cast to the party. His predecessor, Tage Erlander, whom Palme served as an administrative assistant and political adviser, looked the part of the rugged man of the people, big-boned, slow-spoken. He was in the tradition of Per Albin Hansson. In contrast, Palme is slender, speaking

rapidly in English as well as in his own language, quick in his movements.

In theory, LO and the Social Democratic party work in the closest harmony. Critics on the right like to say that they are one and the same. It was soon evident, however, that the prime minister was less than enthusiastic about the Meidner plan despite prodding from the leaders of LO. He took evasive action by saying it would be wise to wait until the royal commission examining the role of employees and the growth of company capital had made its report. That could be the basis for extended discussion and later possibly for action by the Riksdag. This did not satisfy labor nor did it blunt the attack from the right.

The Meidner plan was a central issue in the election debate. But rivaling it in importance was another issue of immediate concern unrelated to the tension between labor and management over control of the economy. That was the development of nuclear energy that would turn the wheels of industry to compensate for Sweden's lack of oil and coal. The concern over the growth of nuclear energy is worldwide. In West Germany it has taken the form of explosive mass demonstrations directed at sites for new nuclear plants, and scarcely less formidable opposition has occurred elsewhere. I venture to say, however, that in Sweden more than in any other country the nuclear factor was a political issue in a national election, and nuclear waste continues to be a major source of confrontation between government and industry.

The reason was above all one man—Thorbjörn Fälldin. The leader of the Center party, who was to become prime minister in the right-of-center government, Fälldin holds what can only be described as a religious conviction of the inherent evils of an age dependent on nuclear power to sustain living standards. A sheep farmer from northern Sweden, Fälldin has an earthy directness and simplicity that seem to come out of an earlier time. As both his critics and admirers have said, he is in appearance

the archetype of the Social Democratic prime minister of
past years.

In conversation, his deeply felt conviction is unmis-
takable. As he said again and again during the campaign,
we have no right to take the responsibility for committing
generations ahead to dependence on nuclear energy with
all its hazards. Deadly radiation from an accident is one
hazard. But the still unresolved problem of disposal of nuclear wastes poses a danger for generations far into a date-
less future, since those wastes have a half life of 200,000 to
250,000 years. And who would control the process, with
plutonium as a by-product? Would it not be a temptation
to produce atomic weapons, although Sweden reached a
decision twenty years before, after extended debate,
against any nuclear weapons capability? Commentators
took certain of his statements out of context. Of course,
they said, there are hazards in any industry. Work in the
forests, an important part of Swedish industry, was an example. But this was a different kind of hazard, Fälldin said.
You could not see it or taste it or smell it, yet it was all-
pervasive. And the peaceful use of nuclear power for electrical energy was in reality a Siamese twin of the manufacture of nuclear weapons.

The newspapers were almost all against his position.
He had to rely on political meetings to put his message
across, and as the campaign progressed he believed that at
least 50 percent of the electorate across the spectrum of all
parties favored the position of the Center party as he expounded it. He said that if he became prime minister he
would depend on the finding of an impartial commission
to determine whether the hazards, and particularly the
problem of the disposal of nuclear wastes, could be miti-
gated, if not resolved. A referendum could follow, and
even a mid-term election following his resignation on the
nuclear issue was not ruled out.

Fälldin's stand was complicated by the views of the
other parties, the Liberals and the Conservatives, which

had formed a coalition with the Center party. They did not agree for the most part with what they considered his extreme position. They believed nuclear power was a necessity if Sweden was to maintain its advanced place in world trade and in living standards. Where was the power to come from, with no natural fuels, if not from nuclear reactors? Fälldin's answer was that the use of power would have to be drastically cut back. This could be achieved by higher rates, inevitably resulting from the great increase in the price of oil. Energy from water power had been comparatively cheap, and this had brought a rapid expansion in the use of electricity. Per capita consumption of electricity in Sweden had become one of the highest in the world. But further expansion had virtually come to an end with this resource exploited to capacity. He pointed out that power from nuclear reactors cost from eight to nine times that of water power. Research into solar, geothermal, wind, and other still untapped sources would be pushed in the hope of a breakthrough.

Apart from the divergent views within the coalition, there was another and far more visible complication. For a country of 8,000,000 people, Sweden with its high technology had already taken a long stride into the nuclear age. Five nuclear reactors were already fueled and in operation and eight more were projected. A sixth was so near completion that it required little more than fueling to begin operation. What would Fälldin do about these reactors already in being? He indicated that he could conceivably compromise on permitting the sixth reactor to go ahead with the production of power, this presumably a concession to doubters within the coalition. But he was adamant in his determination to insure against the hazards of the oncoming nuclear age. Those in the first stages or on the drawing board—the additional seven—would be abandoned. If a commission of experts could not come up with satisfactory answers to waste disposal and the danger of radiation in an accident then the five reactors in operation,

and perhaps a sixth, would have to be dismantled. Surely, said his critics, you cannot expect a commission within a period of a few years to come up with answers that the Americans had been seeking in vain for two decades or more. Dismantling the reactors would be very costly, and with a falling away of electric power it could cause widespread unemployment and even poverty. There was good reason to think that Fälldin did not believe a commission could provide the answers he sought. But the sheep farmer from the north would not budge.

As the election drew near after a campaign as intensive as any Sweden had known in many years, the compromise of the middle way, based on the pact of Saltsjobaden, seemed a piece of remote history. In the Meidner plan the labor movement had taken a step toward nationalization—a radical departure from the welfare socialism that had proliferated in one measure after another for more than forty years. This could mean the kind of polarization that presaged a sharp break with the evenhanded past. At the same time the electorate had been profoundly stirred by the nuclear issue as Fälldin, the evangelist, had carried it to the country. The question in many minds was whether this was a sharp turn in the road separating the old familiar Sweden and a new uncertain Sweden.

4 *The New Broom*

The result of the election in September 1976 was news not only in Sweden but throughout the world. The Social Democrats in power for forty-four years had been defeated by a coalition of right-of-center parties.

This should not after all have been so surprising. The Socialists had been declining in electoral strength ever since the early sixties. They had governed in recent years thanks to the forebearance of the Communists, who refrained from voting in the Riksdag on crucial issues that could have brought the government down. While the Communists had also lost strength, they had retained the 4 percent without which they could not have been on a subsequent ballot.

A close election—with the new coalition getting 50.8 percent of the vote—it was nonetheless proof that Sweden was a viable democracy and not a one-party state. The three parties—Center, Liberal, and Conservative (the last known more recently as Moderate)—had finally been able to collaborate in a national election. They had tried repeatedly in the past and had always failed, as party and individual rivalries made cooperation impossible. They had united behind Fälldin, the sheep farmer, leader of the Center party, who, as a Liberal once described him, was Sweden's Eisenhower, with his sturdy, solid quality, his integrity and honesty. And if one issue could be singled out as the reason for the narrow victory it was Fälldin's intense, unceasing campaign to eliminate the nuclear power reactor option.

The partners in the coalition immediately set out under Prime Minister Fälldin to form a government. With claims from leaders of the three parties it was far from an easy task. A Liberal, Per Ahlmark, was deputy prime minister and minister of labor. Mrs. Karin Söder, a schoolteacher from Fälldin's party, was minister for foreign affairs. Four other women were named to subcabinet posts. Of the 349 members of the Riksdag, 80 are women. The minister of the economy, perhaps the toughest assignment, went to Gösta Bohman, a Conservative, who had taken a vigorous lead in opposing the Meidner plan. A distinguished Liberal, Jan-Erik Wikström, was minister of education and cultural affairs. There was much interest in who would get the post of minister of energy. It was probably inevitable that it went to Olof Johansson, leader of the Center party's youth movement, which is considerably to the left of the party itself. An even more ardent opponent of the nuclear option than Fälldin, he was described as the high priest in the temple in which the prime minister worshipped. As was to be shown later, Johansson's strength in the party was as great, perhaps greater, than that of Fälldin.

Hardly a worse time could have been chosen for a new government to come to power. The worldwide recession, the quadrupling of oil prices, and the competition of Third World countries moving toward industrialization had combined to bring about a sharp drop in the Swedish economy and above all in exports, on which up to 50 percent of industry was dependent. When exports began to fall, the Socialists had initiated a policy of subsidizing surplus production of autos, wood pulp and paper, specialty steels, and a wide range of goods that would be sold when the recession eased. This was expected to come in a relatively short time. It was to be a "soft fall" not too long delayed.

The objective had been to hold unemployment down, with industry keeping on surplus workers or assigning

them to retraining programs and government-sponsored work. As the months passed, surplus stocks built up in one field after another. Several thousand unsold Volvos, some said as many as 10,000, were on the docks of Gothenburg. In a falling market, wood pulp and paper overflowed storage space. Shipbuilding, which had been an important segment of the economy, slumped drastically under the impact of Japanese competition. The figure for unemployment held at 1.8 to 2 percent. But it was a wholly unrealistic figure, since it did not include the retrainees or those on government contract work paid at the going rate. With these categories included, the rate would have been anywhere from 4 to 6 percent, a phenomenally high level for Sweden.

Anyone who expected the right-of-center government to begin dismantling the apparatus of the welfare state would have been quickly disillusioned. Not only was there no move to abolish or curtail principal elements of welfarism, but the new government was to continue to subsidize surplus production in the immediate months ahead. To have had the official unemployment total multiplied two or three times just after taking office would have been a fatal blow for future prospects and certainly for reelection at the end of three years (the Riksdag having reduced the term of office from four years to three). Like the previous government, the coalition was committed to full employment, and it never wavered on the announced policy of full employment. Workers who lost their jobs in the restructuring process were to be retrained, some in heavy engineering in the plants in which they had worked, or they were to be given jobs in state-originated work. This meant that the rate of unemployment would continue to be a nominal 2 or 2.5 percent.

When Fälldin and his minister of the economy began to frame a preliminary budget for the coming fiscal year, however, they were confronted with the dire plight of the national economy. The prospect was for the largest bud-

getary deficit in Sweden's history, about $4 billion. Given the competitive situation in foreign trade, with wage costs plus added welfare measures at a 45 percent increase, the current account deficit in trade was $3 billion. For the first time in this century, Sweden would have to borrow in the international money markets anywhere from $4 to $5 billion. That was to be done, of course, through the Swedish State Bank. The dread was of the "English disease": stagflation, or rising inflation in a stagnant economy.

In Stockholm a few months after the coalition took over I heard a frequent expression, "We have been spoiled for so long." Yet no one either in or out of government seemed to know what to do. The obvious necessity was to cut current consumption. But how to do it? To deprive the citizen of a benefit long taken for granted is difficult and almost certain to produce an indignant reaction recorded in the next election. Already heavily taxed, alcohol and tobacco came in for a tax increase of 15 percent to bring in about $250 million, and the fee for a television permit was upped. Taxes on autos were increased overall by 75 percent, and the cost of electricity in the home was raised by 50 percent. While this was painful for the average citizen, it provided perhaps $260 million, not a very substantial relief for the squeeze on the government.

Nor did the expansion of social welfare benefits cease with the right-of-center government. The annual allowance for each child was to go up by $80 on January 1, 1978. The outlook in the new budget was for an additional 35,000 jobs in the public sector to make up for an expected loss of 30,000 in private industry. And the new government was faithful to the commitment of 1 percent of the gross national product for foreign aid, virtually the only country to reach such a level. Of this, one-third was to go through multilateral channels. By the end of the new government's first full year in office, the nation's international debt would be $7.5 billion, which was about 1.5 percent of GNP. As they scanned the economic skies in the

more social costs

1% foreign aid

West, ministers in the government continued to hope for an end to the recession and an upturn in production.

Waiting hopefully, they faced a struggle over a new annual wage agreement, with demands from the trade unions that would send production costs soaring again. It was such a different Sweden in 1977 from the one I had known. Outwardly it was the same; the streets so clean and orderly with a rush of traffic seemingly unabated by rapidly rising prices, the well-tended parks, the swirling water in the channel between the Palace and the Grand Hotel so unpolluted, so pure that you could drink it, theaters and restaurants crowded. Yet beneath the familiar bright surface was an abyss of uncertainty, and how to bridge it was one of the unknown quantities which at the same time stirred mounting ideological heat. As the deadline drew near for signing a new wage agreement, the threat in the air was of a general strike. As the two sides scurried back and forth with compromise offers and rejection of those offers it seemed a likelihood. At the last minute a year's treaty of peace was signed, and a sigh of relief went up. Negotiated through the intense efforts of Curt Nicolin, head of SAF, the agreement was a big break for the coalition government. The Labor Organisationen agreed to an increase for the year of only 1.7 percent. The negotiation could be reopened in October if inflation had exceeded a certain level. But no one expected this to happen, since inflation was dropping from the double-digit level. In the course of negotiating what was virtually a standstill agreement, Gunnar Nilsson, head of LO, spoke some grim home truths. Addressing the Municipal Workers' Congress in Stockholm he said:

Sweden today does not have the economical growth which could finance an increasing public sector, growing investments, and an improved private standard of living. If one is to increase public consumption, either private consumption or investment must be decreased. If we take

from investment we eat up our future. . . . Part of our
problem lies in the strong economies such as West
Germany and Japan. These economies do not wish to invest in home consumption or public consumption which
otherwise would improve Sweden's chances of export. Today Sweden faces the crisis with decreased private consumption, growing local taxes, and growing foreign credits
which drive us into the arms of the International Monetary
Fund.

This was remarkable realism from one whose main
goal was by the very nature of his office higher wages for
all workers. Looking to the future he called for a systematic industry and economic policy that would stimulate research and technical development. But he was not surren-
dering the future to the concentration of ownership that
had managed through high profits to continue to hold minority power. No, said Nilsson, there was a collective
alternative through employee investment funds promising
a "democratization of economic life." This was a reminder
of the Meidner plan, which was in process of revision for a
second test of voter opinion.

Relief at the wage settlement was tempered, however,
by the prospect of even higher prices. On top of the wage
increase, the value-added tax, covering both food and most
medicine, would go up in July from 10 to 20 percent. It
was hard for even the comparatively affluent upper middle class to take it in. A housewife with something between
awe and indignation in her voice said, "I paid $14 for a
codfish today. Just think of it!" For anything imported and
considered a luxury the price was astronomical. If you
were foolish enough to ask for a Scotch and soda the tab
was $7 or $8.

Here is a dedicated public servant who has spent
much of his career abroad in the foreign service. He has
come back to Stockholm for his retirement. My wife and I,
he says, are living in a two-room flat on the outskirts of

Stockholm. We feel cramped, limited in our choices. We cannot entertain our friends in our apartment, it is too small, and the prices in good restaurants are too high. My pension covers, after taxes, barely enough for our restricted style of living, and so I am going into the small amount of savings I managed to accumulate. Many of my friends are in the same position. This is the reaction of one who sees welfare benefits and wage levels constantly increasing, although they contribute little or nothing to his standard of living.

The prime minister could not escape the contradictions that had emerged during the campaign or the divisions within the government. Nor could he in spite of the recession move arbitrarily to cut back some of the consequences of Sweden's welfarism—a permissiveness, or so it seemed to critics, that had gone a long way toward creating a generous environment.

One privilege contributing largely to the trade deficit was travel abroad. The Swedes are inveterate travelers, and by one estimate they spend $700 million annually escaping from their own dour winter climate. The traveler pays for his airfare, his hotel, and his meals in advance, and he is then allowed to take $1,200 in currency with him for his vacation. In what was hardly a bold step, the government imposed a $5 tax on each traveler. The return from foreign visitors to Sweden is far less than the outflow. I heard several businessmen complain that not enough had been done to build up tourism. The summer season is short, but the complaint was that too little had gone into developing a winter season with skiing and other winter sports. Most of those who come in the off season are the young from various parts of Europe, who travel with backpacks and sleep in youth hostels.

It was interesting to test out individuals in mid-June on where they would spend their vacations. Malta, the young taxi driver said; he and his wife had already made their reservations. Then you can take out $1,200 to spend

as you please? No, $2,400 because my wife also has an allowance. We don't want to go to one of the Greek islands or one of those places in the south of Spain where Swedes talk nothing but Swedish to one another. They are conscientious travelers, too. I was reminded of this in Nanking, when a performance of excerpts from the Peking opera was held up for a half-hour while the interpreter for a group of traveling Swedes explained the plot of what they were about to see.

Weather, the traditional longing for the South, dictates the exodus in the winter months, and it can prevail at other times. In July the weather was abnormally chilly and overcast, and a rush for the South—for Italy, Spain, and Greece—began as though it had been February or March. Needless to say, this is good business for the Scandinavian Airline System, jointly owned by Sweden, Norway, and Denmark, with the Wallenbergs of Sweden the largest investors. It is one of the few profitable airlines, perhaps because the Scandinavians are such determined travelers. Charter flights subscribed to weeks and months in advance bring the price of an air ticket down.

But the principal struggle for the government was in restructuring industries that were in desperate condition because of high wage costs and new competition from Japan and other countries with much lower wage scales. Reports coming in at the end of 1977 were not encouraging. Total profits for companies listed on the Stockholm Stock Exchange had fallen by 90 percent. The gross national product dropped 2.4 percent, and for the first time since 1931 private consumption declined. Svensk Varv, a state-owned shipbuilding company with five big yards, lost $491 million during the year, the largest loss ever suffered by a Swedish company. LKAB, the state-owned iron ore colossus, lost $144 million, and according to one estimate the steel industry suffered a loss perhaps twice that amount. Cheaper Australian and Brazilian ores with lower extraction costs were undermining what had been a bul-

wark of the Swedish economy. Developing countries had begun to produce the specialty steels that once had a high priority in the export market. Similarly pulp and paper, an industry built up over half a century, had operated at 70 percent of capacity. Less costly Canadian and American products had taken a part of this market.

The most severe reverses were being suffered by shipbuilding and steel. Right down until 1975 Sweden was building 7.3 percent of the world's ships—large oil tankers, bulk carriers, and certain specialized ships—in competition with the Japanese. The collapse came swiftly. A state shipbuilding group, Swedyards, absorbed fourteen companies, including such world-famous names as Gotaverken, Eriksburg, and Landskrona. The government had to come up with more than $400 million to nurse the combine through the initial phase, and even then in mid-1978 the losses were stupendous. For 1978 the loss was estimated at close to a half-billion dollars, the largest ever for a Swedish company.

The one company that had elected to stay out of Swedyards—Kockum—was having second thoughts in spite of a government-backed loan of $40 million to cover the financing of two large liquid natural gas ships for stock. Inevitably the cutbacks that came as the scale of the losses became evident—Eriksburg was to close in 1980—meant jobs would suffer. The cabinet determined that more than 10,000 jobs would have to go by the end of 1980 in the state-owned shipbuilding industry. This figure included 1,100 to be dropped at Kockum, still in private ownership. Of the total, according to the cabinet estimate, 6,200 were directly involved with shipbuilding, while an additional 3,000 or more were in subsidiary companies producing marine component parts.

The restructuring of steel was nearly as drastic. Three steel-making companies—Gränges, Stora Kopparberg, and the previously state-owned NJA—were brought together with the formation of Svensk Stal (SSAB). The state hold-

ing company, Statsforetag, has 50 percent ownership in the new company, with the two other privately owned companies each having a 25 percent interest. Statsforetag was given $150 million by the government for its 50 percent ownership in the new steel combine. The unions agreed that the labor force of 18,000 would be substantially reduced. To put the new combine in profitable operation it was estimated that government loans of $1.5 billion over five years would be required. This was for reconstruction and to absorb budgetary losses.

Two cabinet members proving to be among the most able in the coalition cabinet—Minister of Industry Nils G. Åsling of the Center party, and Minister of Commerce Steffan Burenstam Linder, a Conservative—were overseeing these draconian measures. They were working closely with the two industrialists heading the restructured companies. Erland Wesberg, president of Swedyards, had been in the shipbuilding business for more than a quarter-century, having played an active part in building up the shipyards that were, until the crisis, the only real West European challenge to the Japanese. Bjorn Wahlstrom, president of Svensk Stal, was new to the industry, having until a few months before been head of Svenska Cellulosa, one of Sweden's most successful pulp and paper companies.

As the banks issued gloomy forecasts, the realization spread that nothing short of profound changes in the structure of the economy and the standard of living of the consumer could correct the decline and restore stability. The latter remedy would be far from easy. Figures from Stockholm University's school of business showed that payroll costs had increased by 160 percent over ten years. According to the university, this was the highest figure in the industrialized world.

The polls showed the combined Social Democrat and Communist rating at four points above that of the government and the coalition parties. An election at that moment would probably have returned the Socialists with the same

governing majority they had had before, thanks in part to Communist abstentions. Indeed the polls showed that the Socialists might come in with an outright majority. The new broom was falling short of the expectations that arose after the 1976 election. Yet the more informed electorate was well aware that the new government was trying to master troubles deeply rooted in the past. While it might be criticized for not moving faster, the blame for high inflation, subsidized unemployment, the loss of profits, foreign borrowing, and the other ills had much older origins than September 1976.

Per Albin Hansson

The Town Hall, Stockholm

Ernst Wigforss

Ingmar Bergman

Rudolph Meidner

Olof Palme

Curt Nicolin

Marcus Wallenberg

Thorbjörn Fälldin

Olof Johansson

Ola Ullsten

Gunnar and Alva Myrdal

Nils Thedin

5 *The Masters of the New Technology*

As the new government went on with few if any changes in either welfare structure or the policy of subsidized wages to avoid unemployment, the leaders of industry began to speak out. They were disturbed by falling profit margins and the disparity between labor costs in Sweden and in Sweden's best export customers. One of the most cogent and telling presentations was made by Åke O. Liljefors, vice president for corporate environment of ASEA, speaking in a forthright way what was in the minds of many industrialists.

Speaking in 1977 to a conference of electrical manufacturers in Montreal, where ASEA has a subsidiary, Liljefors reviewed the postwar development, which had seen total production volume more than double. Thanks to improvement in industrial productivity the work week had been shortened, and real wages had risen more than 100 percent. Along with the innovative social welfare policies pursued by a virtually unanimous parliament, a corporate tax policy had provided incentives to invest in plant and equipment. One of the historical assets of Swedish industry was organized labor's positive approach to rationalization and its willingness to accept changes in order to achieve higher productivity. Full employment had prevailed for more than thirty years without any significant work stoppages. Per capita gross national product and the standard of living had been among the highest in the

industry critical

81

world. This, Liljefors stressed, was in the broad framework of a traditional free enterprise system, the essential factor being a continuing increase in productivity and a high rate of investment in equipment.

Although the oil crisis of 1973 had coincided with the start of the worldwide recession, the effect had not been felt immediately in Sweden, he said. In 1974 many companies had had record profits, raising the political issue of "excess profits," Liljefors noted, and it was from the exploitation of this issue that he traced most of the country's current ills. Unprecedented increases in wages and salaries under collective agreements for 1975 and 1976 had resulted in a rise in labor costs of more than 40 percent in the two-year period. Swedish labor costs had risen 28 percent faster than comparable costs in important customer countries, he told the Montreal meeting. While this rapid increase was taking place, productivity was declining, going from a 6 percent increase in the previous two years to virtually nothing in 1974 and about 2 percent in 1975 and 1976. Swedish industrial labor costs, including social benefits, were now higher than in any country except Norway, exceeding the hourly costs in Canada by nearly 8 percent. Liljefors hit hard at a facet of the welfare state that had been a source of growing indignation in the middle and upper middle classes:

Another disturbing factor has been a 10 percent rise in employment in the public sector in the last two years at a cost of approximately $1,300 per year to the average Swedish family. At the current rate of increase 100 percent of our population would be in the public sector by the year 2004!

Surprisingly, Liljefors was not negative about the steps that had led to employee participation in the management of industry. As we have seen, a law passed in 1974 required companies above a certain size to have employee

representatives on their boards of directors, and on January 1, 1977, the law of codetermination went into effect, giving workers the right to participate in the decision-making process at all levels of industry.

"As may well be imagined, this new partnership with labor, which is structured in an elaborate system of so-called reference groups and consultative procedures, has imposed serious demands on management in terms of time, money, and manpower," Liljefors said. "With few exceptions the full impact of the law has not yet been felt. May I, however, express the opinion that Swedish executives do not broadly and generally say that this new development is detrimental to the future development of business. It may be but it may also offer new and better opportunities."

Even more influential as a spokesman for industry and its concerns is Liljefors's boss, Curt Nicolin. As head and front of industry, high technology, and the drive for nuclear power, Curt Nicolin is perfectly typecast. Slender, intense, taut, constantly on the move, his face lean, he could hardly be more completely the opposite of the sheep farmer. Besides being chairman of the board of ASEA, Sweden's tenth largest company doing a business of $2 billion a year, he is chairman of SAF, the employers' confederation, and on the boards of a half-dozen other companies. He had a great deal to do with negotiating the 1978 pay freeze, holding wages to a 1.7 percent increase.

ASEA and its subsidiaries produce a remarkable range of heavy electrical products, including railway locomotives and engines for electrical locomotives, gas turbines, conveyor belts, power stations, and, with rapidly advancing technology, transmission systems for high voltage power lines. The company is complex. Of the 44,000 employees, nearly half are in the eleven operating divisions. The others work for the ninety or more active subsidiaries, sixty located outside Sweden. More than half of the ASEA group's sales are overseas. With profits of $151 million in

1976, ASEA was one of the companies that brought the cry from labor of "excess profits" as an incentive to adoption of the Meidner plan. This represented, however, only about 7.4 percent of the turnover.

For seventy-five years ASEA has been an active participant in British industry. Four ASEA group companies have subsidiaries in the United Kingdom for a wide range of production from turbines and marine gears to glass fiber products. ASEA's British factory is at Bletchley, manufacturing drives and control equipment for rolling and pulp and paper mills, fans, pumps, and railway traction equipment. It is not only the oldest but one of the most extensive of ASEA's foreign operations.

Nicolin graduated from the Royal Institute of Technology in Stockholm and took his first job with ASEA's turbine manufacturing subsidiary, STAL Finspang, the original half of what is now STAL-LAVAL Turbin AB. Nicolin saw his opportunity when the company turned to the development of jet engines. He designed ASEA's first jet engine and in his spare time completed the work for his doctorate.

Very early, Nicolin's talents both as engineer and industrial manager were recognized by Marcus Wallenberg, who is Sweden's premier capitalist, with substantial investments in the country's largest corporations. Under Wallenberg's watchful eye, he became chief engineer of STAL's gas turbine department, and three years later he had his first experience of general management when he was made deputy managing director and technical manager. At the age of forty in 1961 he was made managing director of the parent company.

A few months later Wallenberg called on him to make over the Scandinavian Airlines System, which was suffering heavy losses, a source of great unhappiness to the Wallenbergs with their considerable investment in the line. Nicolin's cure is a legend in the Stockholm business community. He assembled all of SAS's 13,000 employees

in an airplane hangar and told them some blunt truths. The company was in a dire financial state, and the only way to make it profitable was to cut back employment by 500 at once. His plain speaking is said to have brought him a standing ovation, and he proceeded to fire the requisite number of employees. An additional 1,900 jobs were eliminated over the next two years, and SAS not only remained solvent but became one of the most profitable international lines, most of the others surviving thanks to generous government subsidies. When Wallenberg stepped down as chairman of the ASEA group, Nicolin replaced him in the top job.

As early as 1971 he was predicting economic doom if the Socialists continued to raise welfare benefits and if wage costs continued to go up to levels beyond those of Sweden's competitors in the world market. He accused the Social Democratic government of squeezing corporate profitability and private saving and of allowing public expenditures to grow excessively, financed by ever higher taxes. Increasingly, he said, this was discouraging industrial expansion. He was pressing for no further tax increases and no expansions of the civil service. Such restraints, he argued, would radically improve industry's prospects.

"The likelihood is that things must become much worse," he said in an interview at the time, "before they become better."

His prophecies as doomsayer seemed belied by what happened between 1971 and 1974. The economy had something like a boom, and between 1971 and 1976 ASEA doubled its turnover and trebled its profits—those "excess profits" that touched off labor's demands for large wage increases. Labor's ire was also aroused by reports of Nicolin's estimated personal income of $360,000 from his various directorships. Here was control of the economy, as Meidner had put it, by approximately 100 individuals of whom the Wallenbergs and their protégé, Nicolin, were the vanguard.

Nicolin was not concerned with technology and industry alone. Having helped perhaps more than any single individual to bring about the wage freeze, he continued to be an articulate advocate of the need for drastic reforms if Sweden was to regain the share of world markets it had before the crisis. In an article in *Dagens Nyheter* with the caption "Dare We Be Realists?" he wrote that in order to recover lost markets prices would have to be reduced in a range of 10 percent. And that, he added, has to occur in an industrial complex that, as a whole, shows no profit, return on capital, or margin—call it what you will:

Profit has become a dirty word in our public debate. But it is unreasonable to expect that *anyone* would engage in industry without anticipation of a surplus. It is even irresponsible. And if we now have no profits the only thing that remains is to cut costs.

Now, then, how can we cut costs? If our costs rise more slowly than those in the world around us, there will gradually be a relative adjustment. Thus wage increases that are lower than those in other countries are helpful. This year's collective agreement in the labor market is helpful. But even this takes time. Rapid results are achieved, for example, through devaluation or reduced employers' taxes. We have devalued the Swedish krona but the trouble in pursuing this route is that it forces up inflation . . .

Large sums have been invested in crisis-ridden companies in order to preserve jobs. But we are not going to restore industry's competitiveness in this manner. Half of the amount used in line with this policy would have meant a dramatic improvement in industry's competitiveness and employment if it had been applied in the form of lower employers' taxes.

Nicolin quoted the most controversial Social Democratic figure out of the past, Ernst Wigforss, as saying that poverty is more bearable if it is shared by all. Can we

change that, Nicolin asked, to: Prosperity is most enjoyable if shared by all?

Nicolin wrote a sharp attack on socialism in *Private Industry in a Public World*. Published first in Swedish, it has circulated in an English translation in a number of countries. Growth in the public sector was a prerequisite, he wrote, for the development of social welfare. That growth has now become an objective in itself. Under the Social Democrats, according to Nicolin, the welfare sector has doubled twice, going from 20 percent to 40 percent of GNP. "It can hardly be doubled for a third time," he wrote. "That would be the end of market-oriented businesses based on private initiative as well as of our present form of society."

The egalitarianism that had narrowed the gap between skilled and less skilled workers was another reason, in Nicolin's view, for the lag in production and investment. The bonus for truly qualified workers is modest, Nicolin wrote; low wage earners should accept the fact that their friends trained in the vocations can earn more than they do. He called for education in business and management and argued that it should not be reserved for high-level executives. Laws that restrict the sale of property to foreigners and prevent the dismissal of employees are a brake on the productivity of the private sector. He quoted a "well-known Swedish Social Democrat," who as early as the 1930s pointed the way things were going, saying: "We're not going to abolish the right of ownership, just make it meaningless."

Nicolin remained, however, confident in the capacity of Swedish industry under free competition. Swedish companies, he wrote, could compete successfully with British, Finnish, and Austrian companies even though wages in Sweden are twice as high. He argued that the low rate of investment had been the cause of the low U.S. growth since the end of the Second World War. He cited among other stimuli for investment the much more liberal

depreciation rates in Sweden that allowed a 60 percent tax-free reserve on inventories. Certainly further stimulation is necessary for U.S. investments to reach the average European level, in his view. An advantage in Sweden was that you knew all the individuals and elements shaping industry. This was unlike the sprawling American system. Politicians and industrial leaders should be able to discuss the nation's goals in an atmosphere of trust and respect, yet more and more there was a polarization between "capitalist" and "socialist."

His associates are sometimes asked whether Nicolin intends to enter politics and promote directly the changes he considers essential to Sweden's recovery. An activist, he would not be content to sit in the Riksdag and participate occasionally in debate. With ASEA subsidiaries in ten countries he is almost constantly on the move, with comparatively little time spent in the company group's handsome headquarters in the center of Stockholm. The company's jet takes him to Paris or London, and then he frequently uses the Concorde. He will spend a day or two in New York and Washington, then a few days in Mexico, where there is a group subsidiary operation, and back to London and Sweden.

Nicolin's interests outside business are pursued with the same intensity. An example is his tennis. He plays the same hard, aggressive game he did twenty-five years ago. Another example is his passion for sailing. Nicolin was the leader of a group of industrialists that put a Swedish entry into the America's Cup race at Newport. While the Swedish boat did not win, it performed creditably.

This was a large gesture in the tradition of the past: Nicolin as surrogate of the Wallenbergs showing how to live grandly. In the context of the present political division and the dispute over Sweden's future, an interesting question is whether men who live exceptionally, beyond the common denominator of welfare and taxation, can survive.

The Wallenbergs themselves are a fascinating case study of past and present.

Old Knut, uncle of Marcus, was at eighty-two the object of a national love-hate relationship. In the Socialist-Liberal press he was pictured as an almost sinister figure dominating the financial life of the nation—a descendant of the legendary sea pirates, with the characteristics of those same pirates. He was opposed to all progress and reform, so the dark picture painted him. On the other side he was a national hero, the intrepid creator of Sweden's industrial-financial strength.

But there was an important distinction between Knut and the later Wallenbergs. He had served as minister for foreign affairs in the critical period between February 1914 and March 1917. This was when powerful elements, including forces in the royal court, believed that Sweden must abandon neutrality and join with Germany, since Germany was certain to win. Knut sternly resisted these forces, which grew in strength as it seemed likely that Germany would capture Paris and win the war. He often battled, with a stubborn resolve, determined elements in business and the social life of the capital. He made many benefactions to Stockholm and the country, including large contributions to the Town Hall, in which he took an almost paternal interest, following every detail with devoted attention.

Marcus inherited the direction of the banks and industries that had been Knut's empire. But he had a more limited view of his own role than his uncle. When he announced that he was moving his legal residence out of Stockholm to a nearby forest to escape high taxes in the city, a storm of protest broke in which all the old accusations were revived. But he was in many ways a traditional Swede. I remember visiting him in the apartment he retained behind the Grand Hotel, which, incidentally, the Wallenbergs own, shortly after his fiftieth birthday. Tradi-

50th birthday in Sweden

tionalism makes the fiftieth supremely important in Sweden. The celebration goes on for days. Around the walls of the apartment were tables piled with gifts of every kind—silver, rare guns, paintings—from friends, employees, and from the royal court. Marcus was so obviously pleased by this tribute. It was later that tragedy struck. His son, Marcus Jr., killed himself in 1971 because, it was said at the time, of overwork and worry about whether he had the ability and the drive to succeed his father. He was forty-seven years old.

No one could question the ability of Marcus Sr. If a single piece of evidence was necessary, it was his choice of Nicolin as head of one of his most important companies. Nor could there be any question of Nicolin's ability. Should exceptional ability have exceptional rewards? One incentive to work as hard as Nicolin works is exceptional reward. If egalitarianism goes so far as to reduce or eliminate these rewards, the adventure of new enterprise could also be reduced or eliminated. By American standards, personal fortunes are not large in Sweden. The net worth of the Wallenbergs—Marcus, nephews, and family—has been put at $30 million. It may be more, but I would guess not very much more. The Wallenbergs live well; their handsome sailing yachts cruise the lovely south coast. This is a source of envy, and envy is a Swedish characteristic, along with the pride that appropriately is called royal pride.

fortunes are small by US standards

Nicolin is a new breed not only in his broad technological background but in his rise from a comparatively modest background to the upper 100, if, that is, critics in the Meidner school are correct in putting that limit on capitalist ownership. For all the worldwide range of his interests, he is a Swede, one can almost say a stubborn Swede. He will use all the resources at his command to try to insure that ownership of the means of production, however much it may have been diluted by the tide of welfarism of the past forty years, remains in private hands.

It is hard to see him as an expatriate, although given his broad international background he could readily find a place in the larger financial-industrial world beyond the borders of his own land.

It is nuclear power, however, that today holds Nicolin's interest both as a practical means of profit for his company and as a bench mark of the advanced position Sweden must hold if the high standards of the past are to be maintained.

6 The Sheep Farmer and the Nuclear Option: The Political Cost

It was the nuclear issue as much as any other that brought Fälldin, the sheep farmer, to the prime ministership at the head of the coalition government. While he had served for nineteen years in the Riksdag, where he was known as a strong debater with strong convictions, Thorbjörn Fälldin had had no experience in the administrative end of government. In the months when the Riksdag was not in session he was normally to be found on his sheep farm at Ramwik in the north, where his close working partners were his wife and daughter. His rugged character was reflected in his simple straightforward manner, his ruddy coloring of one often in the open and not infrequently in harsh weather; this was the image that had contributed to his victory at the polls.

He resembled in some respects the peanut farmer from Georgia, Jimmy Carter. That is true at least of their lack of knowledge and sophistication in coping with the decisions of government in a time of troubles, and it applies, too, to their response to the cutthroat tactics of politics and press. The Social Democratic newspaper *Aftonbladet* ran a savage front-page attack on the prime minister not long after he took office. Expressed in the

form of satire, it foresaw Fälldin committed to a lunatic asylum, the degenerate product of rural inbreeding.

Deeply offended, he held a series of conferences with his chief advisers. Against their advice he stubbornly kept to his initial decision to bring a suit for libel, with damages of one krona, against the paper. Both friend and foe agreed the article was vicious and vulgar, yet they doubted the wisdom of the lawsuit. And their doubts were greater when on the day following publication of the attack, both the publisher and editor ran a front-page apology.

Committed to the suit, his counsel brought the charge of libel, and *Aftonbladet* responded with emphasis on its apology. The verdict was to be handed down at the time the prime minister was due to arrive in Philadelphia for a meeting of Prince Bernhard's Bilderberg group at Princeton.* His first question when he was met by the Swedish ambassador, Count Wachtmeister, was about the outcome. The ambassador's unhappy duty was to inform him that he had lost. The Bilderberg meeting, promoted by Marcus Wallenberg, who accompanied him, was in itself out of character for Fälldin to attend, as he speaks only Swedish. As compensation he went on a fishing trip off the coast of Maine.

If he had put his case to the Press Council the finding would undoubtedly have been in his favor. *Aftonbladet* would have been rebuked and perhaps fined. So deeply hurt had he been by the slanderous article that he let it be known he might resign the office of prime minister. This created a crisis in the government. How would the coalition hold together without his leadership? Would his resignation mean the fall of the government? Or could he be replaced by another member of the Center party? At the end

* The Bilderberg group, started up by Prince Bernhard, is a private gathering of high-ranking officials and influential private citizens from Western Europe and North America who meet informally to discuss common problems.

of a three-week period of uncertainty Fälldin announced he had been persuaded by his wife and daughter that his duty was to remain in office.

"I have asked myself," he told a startled nation, "whether it was worth this price to be in the public spotlight. I am working on the question of how much my family and I should be prepared to sacrifice for the exposed position of a prime minister."

"My family and I have come to the conclusion," he said three weeks later, "that it is possible to live with the tensions of a prime minister's work. I will continue with the job and fight for the things I believe in."

There were less solemn moments when Fälldin's growing political skill in the nation's first office showed to good advantage. Shortly before he left office, Olof Palme had turned over to Fälldin a document that he had received from a former chief of the national police. This was a list of prominent persons who had allegedly patronized a ring of high-priced call girls. Fälldin rose, the document in his hand, and in his grave deliberate fashion told the Riksdag: "I could directly see that this was false. I could state at once that it was false because I found my own name among the listed customers."

The frankness of this statement, its directness and simplicity, brought him a wave of sympathy and admiration from all over the country. Letters, telegrams, even flowers poured into the chancellery. There were skeptics, however, within the coalition who felt he was trading on the image of the honest sheep farmer. It was demagoguery, hypocrisy. Others, both critics and friends, gave Fälldin in the instance of *Aftonbladet* and the call girls credit for a shrewd new tack in Swedish politics, overlooking the issues for the time being for the personal and the human. The reaction from Palme and the Socialists was indignation. Was the future of politics in Sweden to be in the Nixon-American direction of personal vendetta?

More important were the beginning signs of recovery.

For roughly the first six months of 1978 Sweden had a small favorable trade balance. This was due in considerable part to successive devaluations of the krona, which added up to 16 percent. In the process, the unit of Swedish currency was withdrawn from the "Snake," the European currency control device that linked the krona to the deutsche mark and other hard currencies. While it was generally agreed to be a fragile recovery, particularly since the economy of the West continued at a relatively low level, it was nevertheless a hopeful portent. Consumption within Sweden had begun to drop due to high prices and the value-added tax.

So marked was the continuing trade surplus that it was estimated the favorable balance for the year would be $800 million. The great surpluses built up in a half-dozen industries to sustain employment were being melted down, as markets for Swedish exports responded to lower prices, due in no small part to the currency devaluation. Inflation was dropping, too, and the prospect was that it would be around 7 percent for the year, somewhere near the then American figure. Imports were also falling as high prices kept buyers away.

While he was certainly not removed from the pulling and hauling that hopefully would see the economy on a sound course, the outward presence that Fälldin showed his countrymen was one of calm confidence. At the annual conference of the Center party in 1978 in the pleasant city of Eskilstuna, once a major industrial center, he was at his best. The opening session was held in one of the city's parks on a brilliant sunny day in mid-June. With 6,000 or more men, women, children gathered in front of the speakers' stand it was more like a country fair—balloons, vendors of ice cream bars and soft drinks, a relaxed good nature—than a political rally. An interesting feature was the number of women dressed in the native costumes of their respective provinces. One was Mrs. Fälldin—dark-haired, unassuming, never far from her husband's side.

Mrs. Söder, the foreign minister, was a friendly participant, accompanied by her mother, who was in bright pro-
vincial dress. Mrs. Söder must have heard the rumor that if
Fälldin should be unable to agree to a compromise on nuclear reactors she might supplant him as prime minister,
but as she moved through the crowd of the faithful she
seemed completely at ease.

Fälldin opened the rally with a speech of less than half
an hour. He spoke with the simple declarative sentences,
free of any pretension or style, characteristic of his approach to political life, about his hopes for a prosperous
Sweden. At an hour-long press conference afterward at
least three-fourths of the questions bored in on the nuclear
option. Fälldin was not too happy with this interrogation,
but he managed to avoid any firm commitment without a
show of ill nature.

In the late afternoon he was the guest of one of the
Eskilstuna Center party leaders at an informal buffet sup-
per in the garden. In the garden setting in the bright mid-
June sun it was like a scene out of a rustic Renoir. Relaxed,
surrounded by friendly partisans, he could talk about his
future without political rancor. Yes, it might come down to
having to make a choice between living up to his campaign
pledge on reactors or reaching a compromise that would
not violate his conscience. When that would come he was
not sure. But he did not seem unduly concerned about this
decision and what it might do to his own future and that of
the coalition government. Whatever it was—the calm and
the reassurance of his farm in the north, together with his
deep religious faith—he seemed untroubled by the
vexatious choices his divided government would have to
make. This was the assurance that gave him his hold on his
fellow countrymen: the conviction of his integrity.

I had driven down to Eskilstuna with Andreas Ådahl,
the brilliant young adviser to the prime minister on economic matters. A former professor at Uppsala University,
having achieved that honor at a comparatively young age,

he was devoted to Fälldin while at the same time pragmatic about the prospect for a reasonable compromise that would absolve Fälldin from his commitment. We drove back to Stockholm an hour or two before midnight with the sun still hovering on the horizon, the green fields suffused with the light of a gentle sunset. Unmarred with ugly advertising signs, it seemed an idyllic land far from the strife of the contemporary world.

This day had been like the Sweden I had known—a land removed from the bitter strife of ideological conflict. Fälldin was a father figure who conveyed his feeling of affection and concern for all his people as he had done characteristically at Eskilstuna. Was this an illusion? Was it the spell of an earlier and simpler time in a country of remarkable homogeneity that had known no war for 150 years? After I had heard Fälldin, the Center Youth Movement brought the present sharply to mind, voicing a highly critical view of the coalition government and the likelihood of conflict over the nuclear option.

The controversy in Sweden over the nuclear option is without parallel. Elsewhere the dispute has covered particular regions or even neighborhoods. In Japan, for example, so densely populated, the location of a nuclear reactor has been the subject of long and difficult negotiation. In the United States laws in nineteen states prohibit reactors within their boundaries. But in no other country have the government and one of the principal political parties been involved in a prolonged and often confused debate over whether a final commitment should be made to nuclear power.

This is all the more remarkable since Sweden like Japan is without coal, oil, or any other source of energy. The Social Democrats had projected a series of thirteen reactors to supply up to 35 percent of the nation's power needs. Over the years, as the standard of living rose, Sweden had become one of the highest per capita users of electricity. Before the campaign of 1976, as we have seen,

four reactors had been completed and were in operation, a fifth was all but ready, and a sixth was well under way.

The nuclear reactor as built and carried to an advanced stage is an outstanding example of the high technology that has long characterized Swedish industry. Nuclear power has been almost an obsession with Curt Nicolin. Coal and water power as energy sources are both more dangerous to human life than nuclear power, he insists. Nuclear power, he said in an interview not long ago, is both safer and more economical than conventional sources of power. And he believes the industrialized world owes the Arabs a debt of gratitude for forcing a realization ten years earlier than it might have come that energy resources are neither inexhaustible nor completely dependable. A crisis was inevitable, and having come earlier it is more readily solved.

ASEA-Atom is ASEA's nuclear subsidiary. It is owned half by the state and half by the corporation, with the chairmanship shifting every six months from a nominee by the state to Nicolin or someone he designates. Of the first four Swedish reactors, ASEA-Atom built two and Westinghouse two. The performance record for ASEA's two has been superior in continuity and by other measures, according to objective records.

Nicolin has been fired with enthusiasm, and understandably so in light of his long career in technology. He saw the nuclear reactor as the next step beyond the jet in the technological revolution. It has a great potential for sales around the world, in his opinion. Under his direction the design for number eleven in the series of thirteen incorporated all the earlier experience in reactor development, including the safety elements on which so much stress had been put. Although it is not relevant to Sweden since Sweden has never had an earthquake, Nicolin says with confidence that it is earthquake proof. The advanced reactor is said to be years ahead of its competitors, not excluding those in the United States. Inquiries began to

come in from a half-dozen countries. Interest developed in Japan, and a three-way partnership—the Japanese power industry, General Electric, and ASEA-Atom—was formed. The hope is that this will be the pattern for future agreements.

"I fully respect the safety requirements," Nicolin said when pressed on his crusade for nuclear power, "and the importance attached to them in the general debate. If I felt any doubt about satisfying these security requirements I should not work for its continued development."

One reason for his assurance may have been the advanced research ASEA has done to develop a safe container for nuclear waste, resistant to water for hundreds of thousands of years. A press release announced that ASEA had successfully fabricated the first full-scale container for waste. The container was made of alumina powder under a hot isostatic pressing system with temperatures of 1350 degrees Celsius. The resulting material occurs in nature in the form of corundum, which of all existing minerals has the highest rate of resistance to water with a life in an environment of water, according to the claim, of millions of years. The container is sealed with a lid by the same isostatic process to form a joint-free device to hold nearly 150 radioactive fuel rods.

container for nuclear waste

"From the measurements made so far and geological studies it is possible," the company said, "to draw the conclusion that an ASEA container with a wall thickness of 100 millimeters when stored underground in the bedrock can withstand with an adequate margin the effects of the ground water for at least hundreds of thousands of years."

Under intensive research in the ASEA laboratory in Robertsfors in northern Sweden, the high-pressure container was built in record time. There is good reason to believe that ASEA has taken a long lead in the development of a safe disposal process. Lengthy tests will follow before it is a marketable product. But if those tests work out as Nicolin is convinced they will, the commercial possibilities

would seem almost unlimited. It is the kind of advanced technology that has contributed so much to Sweden's prosperity in the past.

Referring to conflict within the government over nuclear-powered electrical energy, ASEA Vice President Liljefors pointed in his Montreal speech to developments by ASEA in this field. ASEA's hot isostatic pressing technique for the safe storage of nuclear waste should be a key factor in a study under way by an energy commission appointed by the Riksdag. He noted that the former Social Democratic government had been committed to the orderly development of nuclear power to relieve the country's heavy dependence on imported oil. Because the Center party had made opposition to nuclear power a dominant issue in the campaign, contrary to the position of the other two coalition parties, strains within the government were eased only in part by a compromise permitting the fueling of nuclear reactors subject to rigid safety regulations. This compromise law did not apply to the five reactors already in operation.

Liljefors felt that polarization of opinion over nuclear power had produced extremes that were unrealistic, as in other countries, notably Germany, where aggressive demonstrators had forced the suspension of nuclear power plant construction. At one extreme in Sweden were those advocating zero economic growth: a society without modern conveniences and a way of living being rejected even in developing countries. Although Liljefors did not say so, this was an approximation of the position Fälldin had taken. With nuclear reactors rejected and a slow and doubtful process before the potential of solar and wind power could be developed, the only choice was to cut consumption drastically.

But a recent survey of those in the sixteen to twenty-four age group, according to Liljefors, had said they wanted to own a car. More than 80 percent wanted as many, or more, energy-consuming appliances as their par-

ents had. Nearly 66 percent wanted to live in a one-family house. In short, a great majority rejected a "back to nature" solution.

The coalition of the center parties that came into power in 1976 was deeply divided on the nuclear issue. A case could be made that they had won the election with a shade under 51 percent of the vote because of that issue as it had been carried to the country by Fälldin. Crusading against the nuclear option in the campaign, he had come flat out against any further development of reactors short of positive proof that nuclear wastes could be safely disposed of. Since the United States had been trying in vain for at least twenty years to find such proof, this was a promise bound to haunt him, in view of the fact that Sweden's reactor program had already gone so far. His passionate sincerity as he had spoken again and again on the perils of a nuclear world was undisputed. But his partners, the Liberals and the Conservatives, simply did not agree with his position, or not at any rate with his extreme view. It had indeed been an extreme view. It might even be necessary, he had said, to dismantle the five reactors already in operation. In that event, the industrialists demanded, where was power to come from to turn the machines that were the basis for the production for export, the heart of Sweden's high living standard? In his crusading zeal, Fälldin's answer was vague and even ambiguous. Other sources of power—solar, wind, geothermal—must be developed. This, however, meant long experimental trial and error, with the prospect for the future years even decades away. People must use less power in their homes, Fälldin argued. But would they be willing to give up the labor-saving devices that had meant so much to householders as the cost of electricity dropped to one of the lowest in the world? The recession in the West had brought a marked reduction in industrial production and therefore a decline in the use of power. But this also meant a drop in employment and a severe strain on the economy. That could

hardly be considered a happy augury for the coalition government.

It was perhaps inevitable that the new government should be marked at the outset by compromise on the nuclear issue. The pressure on Fälldin both from within the coalition and from the establishment of industrialists, bankers, and conservative economists was intense. There was number five fully completed, lacking only fuel to go into operation and contribute to the power grid. Support for Fälldin's hard-line position had declined. Within the cabinet he had the unwavering backing of the Center party's minister of energy, Olof Johansson. Johansson was a concession to the party's youth movement, which was considerably to the left of the party itself. Otherwise, however, the prime minister was a lonely figure, and it was difficult if not impossible to resist the pressures. He gave in, and number five was fueled.

There was reason to believe that public opinion was swinging over to the pro-nuclear position. Within the first two years after the election, the polls showed the Center party dropping from 26 percent of support to 15. It was hardly surprising therefore that as reactor number six came to completion the same internal debate within the cabinet should have taken place. And again Fälldin was prevailed upon to compromise his principles; number six was fueled. The economic crisis was still severe, with unemployment kept from rising to an unprecedented figure of 4 or 5 percent only by active government intervention. When the economy was at a low ebb, the voters would not understand abandoning a project that had cost several hundred million dollars.

But this piecemeal, step-by-step compromise was not viable when numbers seven and eight were ready to go on the line in 1978. The future of the nuclear program was at issue and so for that matter was the future of the coalition government. Immediately at stake was a private transaction between the Swedish nuclear authority and the

Comego Company in France to take the nuclear wastes of the reactors already in operation. That transaction would not be valid until it was approved by the government. It had been hanging fire for some time.

Shortly after the new government had come to power Fälldin had placed considerable confidence in the report of the energy commission set up late in 1976. The prime minister had hopes it would resolve the nuclear dilemma. When the commission made public a final report in mid-June of 1978, it came down for nuclear energy but left open the number of reactors that should be brought into line. The commission had divided 10 to 5, with two Center party representatives, a Communist, and two outside experts in the minority.

The commission majority in a statement "dismissed the thought of winding up nuclear power now. From the environmental and supply point of view, oil and coal are judged to bring with them greater disadvantages than nuclear power. . . . The final position for or against nuclear power ought to be deferred. The commission feels that the ongoing construction of nuclear power plants ought to be fulfilled."

The chairman of the commission, Ove Rainer, said that in his opinion the decision left room for political compromise, but he pointed out that it had the support of a large majority in the Riksdag and the trade unions, which should enhance the possibility of compromise. But as evidence of the fierce emotions stirred by the issue, Rainer said he had never experienced such intolerance and contempt for the viewpoint of others as during the work of the commission. It was obvious that the whole energy situation was not resolved.

This was hardly news to Fälldin. In reply to the majority's statement he said: "It is difficult to grasp which direction the commission majority will in fact give Sweden's future energy policy. Many of the most important decisions regarding nuclear power have been postponed until the fu-

ture. It appears as if the majority has deliberately chosen to be so unclear." Minister of Energy Olof Johansson told the press the final decision would have to wait on the nuclear fuel safety project being carried out under an act of the Riksdag that took office after the victory of the coalition parties.

Here was a confrontation with industry, specifically ASEA, which claimed to have a process insuring the safety of waste disposal that would pass all tests, including the investigations being conducted outside Sweden. But for the prime minister there were those six reactors in full operation, two more complete except for fueling, and the additional five for the initial program of thirteen either on the drawing board or in the early stages of construction. This was the stark reality which the prime minister had to reconcile with his conscience in light of his campaign promise. Industry, above all ASEA, hoped that the issue could be blurred over with a compromise that would permit Fälldin to remain in office while progress on the remaining reactors continued. This might be achieved by dumping Johansson, the chief opponent of the nuclear option.

Speculation filled the newspapers as rarely before. Officials who might have even a remote knowledge of what the decision would be were pursued from office to home. Stockholm had never seen anything quite like the furor over the nuclear option and whether there would be one more compromise. Conjecture and rumor filled column after column as the inevitable decision, due some time during the end of September, drew near. Would the prime minister resign? Would the government fall? Would Fälldin take the issue to the country in a referendum? And who would replace him if he should step down in accord with the deeply held convictions he had expressed in the campaign only two years before?

For the coalition it was a wrenching, anguishing decision. If the center government should lose its credibility after so short an interval, the Social Democrats would re-

turn to power. This was the specter haunting the men and women who had taken office at a time that could hardly have been less propitious. Judging by the polls, they had every reason to be concerned. Support for the Social Democrats at one point stood at 48.5 percent, which meant that, if there had been an election then, they could have formed a government with their own majority independent of the Communists. A handicap for the new government was that the Riksdag, in what was later generally regarded as a misguided move, had amended the constitution to provide a three-year instead of a four-year term in order for national elections to coincide with local elections. Three years was all too brief a time to demonstrate a workable alternative after forty-four years of rule by one party.

In the course of the interminable discussions in the cabinet, Fälldin said he was prepared to resign. He would step aside to be succeeded by Mrs. Karin Söder, the foreign minister and a member of his own party. Mrs. Söder, a teacher with a limited background in foreign affairs, had won high marks in a demanding office that had taken her to many parts of the world. Rumor had for some time predicted that she might be Fälldin's successor. As the discussion grew heated, with her name to the fore as a successor, she was in New York delivering an address to the United Nations and a day later in Washington giving a paper on Africa and the West before Georgetown University's Center for Strategic and International Studies. Meeting journalists and scholars afterward, she gave no hint of the fate that might await her on her return to Stockholm.

Fälldin's partners would not hear of his resignation. It was not that they doubted Mrs. Söder's ability to fill the office, but it would be taken as a confession that the government had failed to resolve a fundamental issue. After additional lengthy discussion and various trials at arriving at a document that would ease Fälldin's conscience and satisfy his partners, a statement was agreed upon and made

public. It was a declaration as ambiguous as the unhappy Fälldin's position. Seeming to say yes to the fueling of reactors seven and eight, it also put in conditions that could be taken as no or maybe if certain stipulations were met at a not too distant date. Signed by Fälldin, Minister for Economic Affairs Gösta Bohman (a Conservative), and Deputy Prime Minister Ola Ullsten (a Liberal), the statement said in a preface that the conditions for fueling two additional reactors—seven and eight—had not been fulfilled in one particular. Therefore permission could not be granted.

The official document went on to declare that, with respect to reprocessing, the stipulation law enacted by the Riksdag had been lived up to. But as to completely safe storage of nuclear waste, the government found that further geological surveys would have to be undertaken before the terms of the law were met. Since the underlying base of the whole country is solid granite, a fact long invoked as a sign of strength, there were those who saw something humorous in what seemed to be an obvious way to square permission with the terms of the law. The statement said:

We want to call attention to the fact that the Stipulation Law does not require that an applicant present information as to the exact location for final storage. The law requires on the other hand that there exist in Sweden an area or areas of a character guaranteeing safe storage in accordance with the law. The necessary geological survey must therefore show that there exists in Sweden a sufficiently large rock formation of sufficient depth and with the other characteristics specified by the security analysis made by the K.B.S. [an ad hoc committee formed by the power companies to present proof that the law had been complied with]. . . . If the applicants having completed such added geological surveys present a renewed application the government will consult the Nuclear Power Inspection Authority. If the Authority finds that

the uncertainty which now exists has been dealt with satis-
factorily the government will accept that the conditions of
the Stipulation Law are lived up to and grant permission to
load [reactors seven and eight].

The statement also announced approval for conclusion of the transaction with France for temporary disposal
of nuclear wastes. It stressed the need for a storage place
for wastes coming from reactors currently in operation.
And plans were disclosed to initiate a control treaty with
Australia in connection with the export of nuclear techniques. The geological tests would take three months before a new application could be made and presumably approved.

So everything seemed to be in order. The government
would remain in power. Fälldin's cherished hope of a referendum was vetoed by his partners. The terms of a referendum could hardly be expressed in such a way as to give voters an intelligent choice on the nuclear option. Reactors
nine and ten were being built. But it was understood this
would be final, and nothing was said of the projected
number eleven. That was made clear by the prime minister
in a press conference after the three-party agreement had
been made public. The most enthusiastic advocate of what
seemed to be an agreed nuclear solution was Bohman,
whose concern was the improvement in the economy and
the hope that the achievements of the coalition in that department would carry the day in the elections in 1979. He
said that the government's formula was 99 percent of the
nuclear solution.

But the comfortable assurance that any weaknesses in
the nuclear posture had been smoothed over failed to take
into account a stubborn enemy of the atom who has never
modified in the slightest degree his conviction of the inevitable peril of a nuclear power system. At about the time
the government communique was being handed out and as
Fälldin was preparing to go on television, his minister for

the holdout

energy, Olof Johansson, was setting his own policy. He was handing out a statement of his personal view that, far from failing to meet only one stipulation that could be readily remedied, the application to fuel the two reactors did not meet five stipulations and therefore could hardly be considered.

With his extensive experience in government, much of it on the welfare-government-intervention side, Johansson at the age of forty-one could be a Social Democrat. Beginning his career as a member of the Stockholm city council, upon his election to the Riksdag he quickly took his place on important committees, including representation for the Riksdag on the board of the Swedish State Holding Company. A member of the national executive of the Center party since 1969, he held a more important post for the exercise of his influence as chairman of the Center Party Youth League. His appointment to the energy post in the cabinet was recognition of his stand, as it complemented that of the prime minister, and his strength with the Center youth.

Johansson's action, taken without consulting anyone in the cabinet, was explosive. Fälldin had gone a considerable way, on television, to support the government's decision. He said that Sweden was the only country in the world where the waste problem was nearly solved. What could be done about the contracts for number eleven, since number ten was the stopping point, would have to be decided by the government. In the uproar that followed Johansson's highly publicized stand, new pressures were brought on the prime minister. He had no choice but to repudiate the minister of energy or, since he had broken the discipline that customarily prevails within a cabinet, call on him to resign.

Even before Johansson's independent stand, the solution proposed in the government declaration had become the focus of political recrimination. Palme called it a camouflaged yes. And what of the promises that had been

made in the campaign on the nuclear option? This was not a geological test boring; it was a political test boring. If the decision were accepted, it might provide a sobering period for consideration of the whole nuclear prospect, which would be welcomed. While this was relatively restrained for Palme, it touched the prime minister at the point of his greatest sensitivity. Indeed, where were the campaign promises?

Although the demands of his partners in the coalition grew ever more impassioned, Fälldin could not bring himself to fire Johansson. This would be an outright repudiation of his campaign pledge to halt the march into a nuclear world. It would also be a blow to the Center party so serious as to reduce its already diminishing strength to a point where it would no longer be considered one of the principals in the coalition.

After nearly a week of struggle within the coalition, Fälldin called a press conference. He had informed the speaker of the Riksdag, Henry Allard, that the government was resigning. There was no longer any basis for cooperation in the coalition and therefore no reason to continue to govern, he said. It was not only the question of fueling the reactors and what to do about a start on number eleven, but the three parties could not agree on a proposed new energy bill. His partners had not completely rejected a referendum, but the fundamental decisions for a meaningful referendum were missing. There is a limit, he said with deep solemnity, to which a party is prepared to sell its soul.

The conservative community was dismayed. Business leaders had counted for so long on a government that would provide an alternative to the Socialists. They had pinned their hopes on Fälldin, "our Eisenhower," for a decade or more. In 1972 one of the most highly respected members of the establishment had told me that at the next election (coming up in a few months) the center parties would show that they could unite to form a government,

and the magic name was Fälldin, the honest sheep farmer. I could only remind him that I had been given this same assurance for many years in the past. But this time you will see, he said, as we skäled over schnapps. They lost that election.

Conservatives, businessmen who take a lively interest in politics, are different from their American counterparts. They are more restrained, reserved, given to a decorum that is partly Swedish formality, partly devotion to business enterprise that is all-demanding. Their private life is private indeed. Foreigners often find this just plain dull. An intense activist like Curt Nicolin is a maverick. But watching the fall of the government on which they had pinned so much hope, after only two years in office, there was nothing they could do.

An immediate scramble began to determine who would govern in the interval before the elections due to be held in 1979. Allard would, of course, meet with the leaders of all parties to try to reconcile their differences. Bohman (a Conservative) put forward a proposal for a minority two-party government (Conservative and Liberal parties) which could become a three-party government (with the Center party) after the electorate voted the coalition back into office on the basis of the marked improvement in the economy. Palme said in a press conference that new elections would be justified, since the government crisis had its roots in the performance of the bourgeois parties. He himself was opposed to a new election, since it would come too close to the end-of-term election one year hence. Nevertheless the Social Democrats were prepared to take the responsibility that the voters would certainly give them. A two-party government would give the Conservatives too much influence, he thought, although here again the Social Democrats were prepared to accept the challenge. A new government should work for the widest possible cooperation around an energy policy.

Not within the memory of living man had the country seen such uncertainty, such speculation and rumor, such recrimination as occurred in the week that followed the government's resignation. The nuclear controversy had struck home to the ordinary citizen. Television had shown how several hundred workers, some of them trained abroad, showed up each morning to operate reactors numbers seven and eight. But with no fuel, there was nothing for them to do, and they were frank to say they did not like accepting pay for idleness. What kind of government was this that allowed such waste to go on with no end in sight? Waiting on the decision of the speaker as he interviewed the leaders of the parties, Sweden had no government. This might happen in Norway and Denmark, plagued by narrow party divisions and extremist fringes, but not in stable, steady Sweden.

Yet it was happening, with the maneuvering, the rivalries, and the jealousies coming to the surface as the press prodded for clues to the outcome. One report was that Allard intended to name a minority two-party government made up of Liberals and Conservatives. Bohman was determined that he and his party should not be excluded in the final choice. He was angry, resentful at the prospect that it might be a one-party government.

But whatever Allard's choice, under the constitution it would have to be confirmed by a vote of 50 percent of the members of the Riksdag, that is, 50 percent of those voting. Palme let it be known that a minority government with the Conservatives would meet with frequent opposition from the Social Democrats, while with a Liberal in the prime minister's office the Social Democrats could be expected to stand aside until election at full term determined the alignment, even though the Center members, the Conservatives, and the Communists might follow party discipline and vote in the negative. The Social Democrats could be counted on to abstain for a Liberal government. With

the abstention of the Socialists and a favorable vote of the Liberals, the requirement of the constitution would be fulfilled.

So on October 12, Allard called on Liberal Ola Ullsten, who had been deputy prime minister and minister for foreign aid in the coalition cabinet, to form a government. With the Liberals having only 39 seats in the Riksdag, scarcely more than 10 percent, it was a narrow base on which to build an administration.

Ullsten had demonstrated exceptional qualities as aid administrator and deputy to Fälldin. At forty-seven he was one of the youngest men to assume the office of prime minister. He did social work and work in the temperance movement at the start of his career before he entered politics to become chairman of the Liberal Party Youth Federation. He was elected to the Riksdag in 1965, holding a variety of parliamentary and party posts. His principal interest has long been foreign affairs and international assistance. Spare, serious in demeanor, he is married to Evi Esko, an engineer, and they have two children. He would need all his parliamentary experience and skill in the months ahead, notably in steering the complex energy policy bill to passage.

Standing before the Riksdag with his sober, earnest demeanor—professorial is how he is often described—Ullsten delivered the policy statement of his government. It was a careful, shrewdly drawn document calculated to stir the least opposition. By inference at least, it recognized that while the development of nuclear power would be continued, the difficult task in the months ahead was to evolve an energy policy acceptable to the principal parties. In some respects the task of the Ullsten government, with a parliament deeply divided, was like that of the Carter administration in trying to achieve a majority for an energy bill. On energy the Ullsten statement was a broad generalization, yet it could be interpreted as a go ahead for the nuclear option:

Energy policy must be aimed at catering for energy requirements, achieving more efficient energy conservation, developing new renewable sources of energy, reducing Sweden's heavy dependence on oil, and giving freedom of action for the future. This government intends to pursue an energy policy which can gain wide support in this House and among the Swedish people. This government will work to intensify the security requirements imposed on different types of energy. This government considers one of its foremost tasks to be that of enhancing the security and reliability of our energy supplies. The concern felt by many people over the hazards of nuclear power and other types of energy should be taken by us as a call to establish the greatest possible measures of security.

It was the kind of statement into which all factions could read their own hopes. At the same time it left the possiblity of a broad consensus for future consideration. Somewhat the same approach was accorded the social policy of the new Liberal government:

The work of the new government will be founded on the ideas of social liberalism which the Liberal party has long propounded in the Riksdag and in the tripartite government which was formed in 1976. This government's proposals can only be realized if they obtain the support of a parliamentary majority and we shall endeavor to establish our policy on the broadest possible basis.

Underlying our work will be an endeavor to build society upon the initiatives, responsibility, and idealism of its members. Diversity and the market economy are to be combined with social care and justice.

The market economy of our society is to be reinforced through measures which will increase competition and counteract the concentration of power. In a climate which is generous to enterprise, small and medium-sized firms will be able to make important contributions to the development potential of the entire economy.

Recognizing continued widespread complaint about the lack of sufficient day care centers—an issue in the 1976 election—the new prime minister acknowledged that a "satisfactory fabric" of child care had not been achieved. And, he added, we are still a long way from arriving at equality of status between men and women at home and in working life. Sweden was in many ways a good society, having created security and affluence, but it was, Ullsten told the parliament, still a long way from being a perfect society. The system of taxation had to be reformed, for example, and marginal tax rates reduced.

Whatever else the one-party government might achieve in the eleven months of its tenure, the nuclear compact was sealed. Reactors seven and eight would be fueled and put in operation at the earliest possible moment. The progress already made in planning and initial construction of nine and ten would be pushed. And there was little doubt that eleven would be carried through, with twelve still undetermined. It was unlikely, indeed all but impossible, that parliamentary intervention could interrupt the nuclear course. It was the program of the Social Democrats that was being carried out. The only visible opposition at this late stage would come from the Communists and perhaps from the Center party representatives, with Johansson in the lead. Fälldin was so downcast by the turn events had taken that he proposed to retire entirely from politics and devote himself to his sheep farm in the north. But his partners in the coalition dissuaded him from such a drastic step, pointing out that with his retirement from the Riksdag Johansson would be the ranking member of the Center party in the parliament, and that would be unfortunate for the party and for an energy policy.

It is a curious irony in light of the political furor over the nuclear option that Sweden should have the largest uranium deposits in Europe. Near the town of Skövde in the west the deposit covers more than 200 square miles. This is 80 percent of Europe's reserves. The uranium is

low grade, so that it takes about 900,000 tons of ore to get 120 tons of processed uranium. Development did not begin until the 1960s; it is being carried out by LKAB, a state-owned mining company, in cooperation with two other companies.

Between 1965 and 1969 LKAB extracted 200 tons of uranium in a demonstration plant at Ranstad. Ambitious plans are projected for a full-scale operation of a million tons of shale a year that would produce, besides uranium, molybdenum, aluminum oxide, nickel, phosphorus, and vanadium. The goal is to produce 400 tons of uranium annually. The government is allocating $10 million for the advance project, which is still some distance in the future. Sweden's own uranium would presumably be sufficient to fuel Swedish reactors, with a balance for export.

* * *

Fälldin's coalition government had been a curious interlude. The Greek temple that is the chancellory, where I had seen one prime minister after another over the years, had failed to provide a comfortable environment for the leader of the Center party. Whether it was modesty or the straightforward cast of his mind, he had been uneasy with the exercise of power. Or the real difficulty may have arisen not with Fälldin himself but with the strains within a coalition government. That the center parties had failed to offer a viable alternative few would dispute. So much had been hoped for after the 1976 election, which ended forty-four years of domination by the Social Democrats. The gloomiest prediction expressed privately by the centrists was that failure meant the Social Democrats would return to office and hold power until the end of the century.

One reason for the dour predictions was the new image that Palme presented. He had been thought of during 1976 as a demagogic figure with little regard for the proprieties of Swedish politics. One thing Palme never lacked was self-confidence. My wife and I had the last talk

with him in the chancellery on the day of his retirement following the defeat of his party in the election of 1976. Discussing a wide range of subjects and taking frequent telephone calls, he seemed completely at ease. He was looking forward to an extensive tour of southern Africa on a mission for the United Nations. As we left at the end of two hours, just as Fälldin was coming in through another entrance, Palme's parting words were, "When you return you will see me again in this office." We saw him a year later in New York as he was preparing for a long evening with sympathetic Americans on the left. He had the same insouciance, the same belief that he was moving with the winds of change.

Many remembered his debate with Fälldin in Gothenburg, during the 1976 campaign, when he had drawn the roars of the crowd of thousands in the auditorium. But those watching on television had been offended by his histrionics, so in contrast with Fälldin's serious discussion of the issues. Something of his early reputation prevailed during his first months in opposition, a role hardly congenial to his brilliant, dynamic temperament. He had emerged from the crisis seeming more mature, more sober, showing his concern for the plight of his country as well as his party. Moreover, at the annual conference of the party he had skillfully directed certain changes to meet discontents long expressed. As one example, officeholders in positions in the party executive were replaced in several instances, despite complaints, by women who felt they had been discriminated against at the top level. And this was particularly important considering the large numbers of women in the work force, perhaps 50 percent of the total.

Looking to the more distant future there was discussion among veteran Socialists active in the party and in the Riksdag of a possible coalition with the Liberals. The latter would not go along with anything as radical as the Meidner plan. But recognizing the urgent need for new

sources of investment, they might agree on a plan for pooling a share of profits with a share of wages in a formula that would not seem to mean nationalization. Government by a Liberal-Social Democrat coalition would mean government by skilled technocrats, with ideological content at a minimum.

For Ullsten his first task, picking his cabinet, was far from easy, since he had only 39 members of his own party in the Riksdag to choose from. There is a tradition, however, of nonpolitical specialists serving in cabinet posts. The new prime minister retained from the previous cabinet Sven Romanus, a nonpolitical appointee, in the justice ministry. Retained also was Jan-Erik Wikström, a leader of the Liberal party, for education and culture. To foreign affairs and foreign aid he named Hans Blix, a nonpolitical civil servant who had been serving as a deputy to Mrs. Söder and had experience in the U.N. Six women were appointed to cabinet and subcabinet posts. For a new ministry responsible for wages, pensions, personnel development, and organization, he named Marianne Wahlberg.

In the vote of confirmation in the Riksdag, the Communists and Conservatives voted in the negative, while both the Social Democrats and the Center abstained. This was sufficient, with the Liberals casting 39 votes in the affirmative. Bohman accused Ullsten and the Liberal party of treason for agreeing to form a one-party government. To observers this seemed to suggest the pattern of the future, the extremes of left and right opposing a center government standing firm for the reforms of the past forty years. Under the most difficult circumstances, the three-party coalition had sustained those same reforms with only minor modifications. The continuing improvement in the economy seemed to ensure that the cost of welfare, together with a wage level that was still high when compared with other industrialized nations, could be borne. While inflated prices had eroded the standard of living, it was one of the highest anywhere. And the goal of a society of

economic justice, with the gap between the affluent and the poor narrowed still further, had not been lost sight of.

The short-lived agreement by the three coalition partners on the nuclear option contained a promise by the government to pursue actively questions of security control in the framework of INCFCE, the international organization for fuel cycle evaluation. The United States actively supports INCFCE, and the Soviet Union and thirty other countries are members. How much it means as the major European powers go in for fast breeders is questionable. The Soviets have been reported preparing to sell such a reactor to Libya, which somehow hardly seems compatible with stability and nonproliferation.

Far from standing alone in recognition of the nuclear hazard, Sweden, with aggressive industrialists such as Curt Nicolin, will be part of the new world; it is a world bound to expand with a power undreamed of a short time ago.

The Swedes have only to look at their neighbor Finland to see how fast is the rush toward nuclear power. At the town of Loviisa a Soviet-built nuclear reactor was in operation in 1978, and a second, 100 yards from the first, was nearly completed, with 600 Soviet workers still on the job. Talks are going on about a third plant which, with a capacity of a million kilowatts, will be twice the size of the 440,000-kilowatt plant now in service. Executives of the Imatram Voima Power Company, owned by the government, are said to be confident that a final agreement will be reached with the Soviets to build this plant. Both Westinghouse and Sweden lost out to the Soviets in their bid to Finland for construction of a nuclear reactor. Moscow loaned the Finns money at a low interest rate, gave them a year's supply of uranium free, and let at least half of the work be subcontracted out to Finnish firms.

The Soviet contract requires each contracting country to turn over all nuclear wastes to the Soviet Union. So far Soviet nuclear plants have been exported to East Germany, Poland, Bulgaria, and Hungary. But Moscow

[handwritten margin note: Soviets export of nuclear plants]

lost out to Westinghouse for a plant in Yugoslavia and to a Canadian firm for a reactor in Romania. The Finns are confident that the Soviets will do extremely well in the nuclear market. Far from being concerned about the hazards in the type of reactor now being built almost everywhere, they are going directly into the fast breeder that uses plutonium and then out of the cycle produces more plutonium. It is the fast breeder that President Carter has sought to restrain for the obvious reason that the amount of bomb material is far greater, and, with nuclear proliferation, the peril of a nuclear war or terrorist seizure is thus multiplied many times.

Fälldin and his minister of energy made a valiant effort to stem the tide, but it was too late even before they took their stand. Their fears—an accident taking thousands of lives, an accidental nuclear explosion triggering a war of nuclear annihilation—may prove groundless. Man has ventured into an era about which little is known of the ultimate consequence for the fate of planet earth and its inhabitants.

7   *Sweden and the World*

In its relations with the rest of the world as much as in its internal affairs, Sweden has sought a middle way—neutrality in war, aid to those who need it in peacetime. Abroad as well as at home, it has been determined to live up to the standards set in arriving at a middle way, though preachments on foreign policy by a small power in the north of Europe have often sounded self-righteous. Much of its policy has been concentrated on the division between the industrialized West and the Third World, and with it have gone large sums of aid—large for a nation of 8,000,000 people—to try to raise standards in the developing nations and particularly in agriculture. The cornerstone was neutrality, strict and unyielding.

In the First World War neutrality caused severe hardships. But the three countries in the Scandinavian peninsula were united in a determination to stay out of the conflict. The strain in that earlier time was nothing like that which Sweden felt after the spring of 1940, when Norway and Denmark were occupied by the Nazi forces while Finland was engaged in a heroic struggle with the Russians.

Given the close ties in trade with Germany, the pressure from Hitler's Reich to come in on the German side was intense. The German connection, as it had existed during the years of rearmament and then in the war, deeply troubled the Swedish conscience. How could it be that a

nation so devoted to equality and justice should have been a party to the rise of Hitler's might? The answer, of course, was the necessity for trade with a trading partner of many years standing. And there were those on the right in Sweden who saw the Nazis as the winning side. A small minority, they were nevertheless vociferous in a segment of the press.

The structure of neutrality, buffeted as it was from 1940 to 1945, was unyielding. It was grounded in a four-party coalition government that came into being on December 1, 1939, the day after the outbreak of the Finnish-Russian war. In that government the Social Democrats had five seats and the bourgeois parties—Liberal, Agrarian (later Center), and Conservative—two each. The Social Democratic prime minister, Per Albin Hansson, read the program of the government in the second chamber of the Riksdag on December 13, while Gösta Bagge, the new ecclesiastical minister and leader of the Conservatives, read the program in the first chamber.

When the Skagerrak blockade was instituted with the invasion of Norway and Denmark in April 1940, Swedish imports were reduced by approximately one-half and exports by about one-third in comparison with the average volume of 1936-38. The importation of food was drastically decreased, which meant severe belt tightening and ultimately a wage and price freeze to curb rising inflation. Domestic sources were sharply limited by a drop in the importation of artificial fertilizers and fodder. A shortage of labor resulted from full mobilization. Defense costs rose from $62 million in 1939 to $500 million by the end of the war. While Sweden's insistence on strict neutrality often sounded smug and self-righteous to the rest of the world in the cauldron of war, it was maintained with great difficulty for the five years of the conflict. The determination of the government to stand firm and united was expressed by the Social Democratic defense minister, Per Edwin Sköld, in a long speech in the Riksdag:

Sweden is the point of departure for all of our efforts. Without an independent Sweden, our efforts are ended. If we wish to improve social conditions, if we wish to work for peace on earth, if we wish to create a society that is better in this or that respect, then first and foremost we must have a free place to work where we can make full use of our powers. This place is Sweden, and in order to preserve it there is in fact no limit to the sacrifices we ought to take upon us.

If the physical sacrifices were severe, they were as nothing to the psychological strains that were intensified with the spread of the war. At the outset of the first Finnish war a newspaper printed a report on February 16, 1940, that a request by Finland for military intervention had been rejected by the government. That same day the prime minister reported that an inquiry had been presented by Finland's foreign minister and the answer given had reasserted Sweden's neutrality. Because the reply had seemed brusque and unfeeling for neighbors with such close ties, it caused considerable agitation. This was softened by King Gustav V, who intervened a few days later with the same conclusion but expressed it in much gentler words. He said that it was with "sorrow in my heart" that he had reached the same decision as the prime minister on the position to which he, the king, had previously subscribed. He said that Sweden was trying to support "our neighbor Finland's heroic battle against the superior power." When J. B. Johansson, the leader of the Conservatives in the first chamber, delivered his obligatory loyalty declaration, he said that he did so not in support of the government's policy but of "His Majesty the King's proclamation."

A graver and more troubling test came when the Nazis attacked Russia. Germany demanded the right to transport troops from Norway to Finland on Swedish railways. On information provided by the government, a long de-

bate ensued in the Riksdag. What only became known much later was that the prime minister and the foreign minister had already informed the Germans that the answer would be affirmative and they could proceed to make their plans to move the Engelbrecht division. As the Swedish scholar Karl Molin wrote:

> While the members of the Riksdag sat on the express train to Stockholm (on the way to a special session to consider the German request), technical negotiations between the Swedes and the Germans had already been started. In comparison with earlier foreign policy crises, the events at mid-summer 1941 meant that the Riksdag had become a piece on the chessboard but, as previously had been the case, it could not affect the game's outcome. The real difference seems to have been that the government considered a formal hearing of the Riksdag to be a prerequisite this time so that its members would feel themselves bound by the decision and obligated to defend it publicly.

In May of 1943 I was one of five American newspapermen invited by the Swedish government to visit Sweden. The informal leader of our group was Raymond Clapper, the Scripps-Howard columnist, who had a wide following in America. Flying from Aberdeen in Scotland across the North Sea was hazardous, since the air space was frequented by German fighter planes and no cover would be provided for a Swedish aircraft of the Scandinavian Airlines System. We had spent some time in blacked-out Britain, and it was a surprise, indeed a shock, to come over the brilliantly lighted city of Stockholm. The Swedish capital was the only one, with the exception of Madrid and to a lesser degree Lisbon, on the periphery of the war, to be carrying on normally.

The bright, outwardly normal front was slightly unreal. The contrast between blacked-out Britain and America, rationed and with many millions in uniform or in

war plants, was too great. The Swedish-American Society gave us a banquet, nearly a thousand diners in the ballroom of the Grand Hotel. The friendly speeches had a familiar ring and so did the skäling. The Swedes are a formal people, with formality turned up to the top level on such an occasion. Presiding was Count Folke Bernadotte, with a royal prince and princess present as guests of honor. Acting as mediator for the United Nations in 1948, Bernadotte, a nephew of the king, was shot down by terrorists in Jerusalem. I have a vivid memory of the aftermath of that banquet. The prince and princess invited us to their rather modest apartment for "a drink." The drink lasted until the early hours of the morning, when polite police informed us that neighbors had complained about the noise.

While the surface was outwardly normal—the cafés crowded, men and women in evening dress, streets brilliantly lighted, we were quick to realize that beneath the surface deep strains and uncertainties, the humiliation of having to yield to one German demand after another, had exacted a high price. At the time of the crisis over the German demand to send troops from Norway to Finland, the coalition government had been threatened by opposition so strong as to raise, briefly at any rate, a question about its existence. Four leading Social Democrats had taken a strong position in favor of a negative answer to the German request. During a debate within the Social Democratic party it was proposed that the bourgeois parties be approached with a request for cooperation in refusing the request. Per Albin carried the day by arguing that if the other members of the coalition were opposed, then the Social Democrats would go along in the interest of unity and neutrality. However, the Liberals, the Agrarians, and the Conservatives, with some dissent in their ranks, accepted the decision reached by the government.

The most humiliating concession was for transit traffic between Norway and Germany across Sweden. The demand had been made while fighting was still going on in

Norway, and Sweden refused on the ground that this would be a violation of Swedish neutrality. When the fighting ended in June, with Norway's feeble defenses swiftly overwhelmed, the request was renewed, and the government in Stockholm could find no reason to refuse. One daily train each way took German soldiers home on leave and back, with Swedish military guards on the trains while they passed through Swedish territory. The Germans were prohibited from carrying arms on these leave trips. It was, for an American, a curious sensation to watch at a level crossing near Gothenburg a train moving to the north. Several German soldiers seeing spectators mockingly held up the Churchill V for victory sign.

Although Allied sentiment in Sweden in the summer of 1943 was estimated at 90 to 95 percent, the harsh fact was that Sweden was dependent on Germany for its industrial existence. The highly organized and efficient Swedish industry could not run without several million tons of fuel supplied by Germany. In return the Swedes were shipping what the British charged was 250,000 tons of war materiel in 1941, more the following year. Much of this was iron ore. Swedish shipments supplied as much as 20 percent of the ore Germany required in 1941 and perhaps more in 1942. But the ratio was greater because of the richness of the Swedish iron. It was not only from Britain and American that protests came over this traffic with the Nazi war machine. Courageous newspapers such as the Gothenburg *Handels Tidningen* kept up a constant editorial attack on the trade with Germany. The British press carried a series of articles putting the total traffic at a figure the Swedes said was greatly exaggerated. Not only ore but ball bearings and other finished products for the German war machine were part of the exchange, according to the British articles. At the same time, on the level of public opinion, there was one manifestation after another of understanding and sympathy for the Allied cause. John Steinbeck's *The Moon Is Down* drew packed audiences in leading thea-

ters. William Shirer's *Berlin Diary* sold 100,000 copies in Stockholm alone.

A never ending reproach to the Swedish conscience was the plight of their brothers and sisters in Norway, Denmark, and Finland. After more than three years of occupation, the diseases of malnutrition were widespread in Norway, where the hardships were more severe than in Denmark. Swedish business men occasionally allowed to visit Oslo reported that, while outwardly the German occupiers were behaving correctly, repression and violence were close at hand. At least 35,000 recruited for a labor battalion were subject to martial law. Without any warning the occupiers could take over a household and order the occupants out by noon of the following day, leaving all possessions behind. What Norwegians dreaded most of all was arrest and deportation to Germany, where torture and probably death in a concentration camp awaited them. The faces in the long bread lines that formed each morning to get a partial ration were drawn and bleak, etched with hunger and fear.

Although the Norwegian government-in-exile in London was resentful and even bitter over Sweden's neutrality, the Norwegians under the Nazis were thankful for an escape hatch. Despite every measure taken by the Gestapo, as many as 30,000 to 35,000 escaped into Sweden. Many were leaders in the underground resistance to the occupation, who passed back and forth; one leader is said to have crossed and recrossed thirty-five times. A ten-month-old baby was passed from one outpost to another to be forwarded once in safety to his mother in Stockholm. It would be impossible to exaggerate the courage of those who passed back and forth. This is largely an untold story. A zone about fifteen miles wide strung with barbed wire and planted with occasional land mines extended along almost the entire border. Merely to be caught there meant death. Risks were taken daily, quite apart from the border crossing. Copies of *The Moon Is Down* circulated from

hand to hand even though possession was almost certain to mean forced labor or even death. Morale, a common front among high and low, was reported good even though in the beginning of the fourth year time passed with interminable slowness in cities and towns totally darkened as the long awaited Allied invasion seemed doomed never to come.

The Norwegian legation in Stockholm set up an elaborate organization to care for the influx of refugees ranging from 100 to 400 a week. Many were in serious condition, suffering from stomach ulcers and malnutrition. Their care was financed by the Norwegian government-in-exile in London. Those who were able were later given jobs in the forests, where the labor shortage was acute because of the number of men under arms and the greatly increased use of wood as fuel in converters for motor cars. The universities, Lund and Uppsala, took in many Norwegian students, 800 at Uppsala alone, in university and preparatory courses. The desire of the young was to get to England and into uniform, but because of the great shortage of air space only a few thousand succeeded in joining their fellow countrymen fighting with the Allies.

To the south of neutral Sweden, the situation in Denmark was quite different. In that pocket handkerchief size country on Germany's border, the Nazis had set out to create a docile fiefdom as a demonstration to the world that their occupation was benign and even welcome. But the Danes resisted with a high degree of effectiveness and with the subtle humor that is so much a part of the Danish temperament. Bewildered and confused by their swift engulfment on April 9, 1940, the Danes accepted at face value certain promises made by the Germans. This led eventually to the formation of a coalition government built around Eric Scavenius as foreign minister. A reactionary pro-German but not pro-Nazi, Scavenius was one of the realists who believed Hitler would win and therefore it was necessary to deal with the Nazis. After considerable soul-

searching, even the Labor party agreed to representation in a government that was to rule Denmark throughout the war.

Under the threat of dissolution by parliament, the Scavenius government resisted major German demands. The first was to join actively on the side of the Nazis. The second was to allow Danish workers to be transported to forced labor in the Reich. In principle this was refused, although at one point about 35,000 Danes were working in Germany. They were treated as equal to German workers, with social security and other benefits, and were allowed to send funds back to their families. As the third year passed and German manpower became seriously depleted, the occupiers made an attempt to recruit 100,000 "volunteers" for work in the Reich, but with the resistance of the government this had little success.

In the autumn of 1943 the rumor spread that the Nazis intended to round up the Danish Jews and deport them to concentration camps in Germany. The number was comparatively small, many of them elderly Jews whose families had lived in Denmark for generations. As the rumor seemed to be confirmed by preparations reported by the underground out of the German high command, secret plans were made for a rescue operation. It was executed with such success that thousands of Jews escaped by night across the Øresund to Sweden. The number has been variously put at from 6,000 to 11,000, the figure including a small proportion of non-Jews threatened by deportation or death. The whole operation was one of the most successful in the annals of escape, organized with skill at both ends of the operation.

Throughout the war, not only Norwegians but hundreds of other refugees—Russians, Finns, Poles, Balts —found safety in Sweden. The Russians and Poles managing to escape from forced labor camps across the northern Norwegian border were often in desperate physical condition. They were given medical attention and housing on ar-

rival. It was a safe haven for all regardless of race or creed, and this had to be weighed against the resentment felt toward Sweden's neutrality and the continuing trade with Germany.

As the war was ending, Sweden confronted the painful problem of finding new terms of cooperation with her Scandinavian neighbors who had suffered so terribly. Throughout the war, the haunting specter had not been Norway, since the belief was that the old ties could be renewed once the fighting stopped, but Finland. The deep-seated fear was that Russia would take over once the Nazis were defeated and driven out, thereby putting the Soviet Union on Sweden's borders. Tremendous pressure had been built up in March 1940 to compel Sweden and Norway to allow the transit of British and French troops to Finland. This was during the Soviet-German pact and after the heroic stand of the Finns in the winter war had won worldwide acclaim. Sweden's refusal stirred angry resentment, particularly in the United States, where the drive had been sparked by publicists with passionate ardor for the Finnish cause. If Sweden had yielded, it is hardly necessary to add, the entire Scandinavian peninsula would have been occupied at once, and the course of the war would have been quite different, especially since neither Britain nor France was prepared with battle-ready divisions for a rescue operation in Finland. Furthermore, it would have sealed the enmity of the Soviet Union, which would have been a fatal obstacle to the collaboration among the Allies after June 1941 that finally brought down the Nazi war machine.

With the German conquest of Finland, tensions somewhat eased. Yet as the war ground to a close there was the fear that the Soviets would take over Finland as they had absorbed Estonia, Latvia, and Lithuania into their empire. Although the Finns had an estimated 300,000 combat-experienced troops against the roughly 90,000-man Nazi occupying force, the fear was that any attempt to break

free of the Nazi embrace would very likely mean Russian intervention. While peace did not bring the worst, the Finns were forced to cede the Karelian peninsula and two ports to the Russians. Reparations added up to $444 million. Subsequently, under the skilled and courageous leadership of President Urho Kekkonen, the Republic of Finland was able to sign a mutual defense agreement with the Soviet Union that kept the Russians at arm's length while the reparations debt was paid off in a remarkably short time by the hard-working Finns. An effort by Sweden to form a pact with Finland was quickly vetoed by Moscow.

There could be few illusions in Sweden as the war was ending about the difficulties in uniting the Scandinavian countries in another Nordic Union. Prime Minister Nygaardsvold of the Norwegian government-in-exile had declared in a speech in London that a union of the Nordic states was not part of Norway's postwar plan. The sentiment in London was for a continuing close relationship with Britain. The Nygaardsvold speech came as a shock to Sweden, where the hope of a Nordic Union with much closer ties than in the past had been cherished. Others, including Östen Undén, former foreign minister and later chairman of the parliamentary foreign relations committee, argued the need for a Nordic bloc but said at the same time that it should be part of a larger international organization. In an enviable position, as the rest of industrialized Europe had been ravaged by the war, Swedish newspapers were fond of saying, "Swedish industry will win the peace." This was unlikely to win friends among Sweden's neighbors, where the cost of the conflict had been so high.

Sweden had about 800,000 men under arms, many of them highly trained in what was known as "the winter war in the woods." This was a remarkable number for a nation of 8,000,000. A rearmament program costing a billion dollars was initiated at the end of 1941, projected to carry into the peace. While there could be no doubt of the ultimate

outcome, either Russia or Germany would have paid heavily in casualties for an attack on Sweden; even though de-
fensive planes were few, Swedish forces were skilled in
techniques particular to a country in defense under snow
for so many months. This was unquestionably a factor in
Sweden's adamant neutrality. It is possible that as the
sacrifices of the military burden bore down, the strength
of the Swedish military was exaggerated. The contrast with
the pacifism that before 1940 had reduced Norwegian and
Danish defenses to a mere token was a source of pride.

The painful decisions that neutrality had involved and
the sense, it may have been guilt, of Sweden's good for-
tune were to condition the postwar attitude toward the
world beyond Sweden's borders. The big powers were in-
herently evil, in this view. They used their power for their
own selfish ends. This attitude had not a little to do in a
subsequent crisis with the United States, when in response
to outraged Swedish opinion relations were frayed almost
to the breaking point. So much that had happened during
the war could be put down to the accident of geography
and to Germany's continuing need for iron, which matched
certain of Sweden's vital needs. Without Swedish fortitude
and Swedish resolve, the outcome might have been far less
fortunate. But dire necessity had a great deal to do with it.

In the last year of the war Sweden had trained both
Norwegian and Danish refugees in a police force intended
to take over once the Germans had surrendered. On May
5, 1945, the Danish brigade arrived in Elsinore to be
greeted by cheering crowds. At the same time the Norwegian force reached Oslo. They were to maintain order until
the respective governments could assemble and equip
their own armies. Sweden's action helped to alleviate the
resentment and hostility growing out of the contrasting
fate of the three powers.

But the differences between neutral Sweden and the
two nations that had been subject to the rigors of a terrible
war could not be easily bridged over. As Sweden reached

out for world markets, her industry more or less intact, recovery in Norway and Denmark came slowly. The Danes hoped in the immediate postwar era that an open break between East and West could be prevented. But then came the events of 1947 and 1948 that shattered these hopes: the Soviet opposition to the Marshall Plan and the Communist coup in Czechoslovakia. While the Allied propaganda on Soviet participation in the war, for example the heroic stands at both Stalingrad and Leningrad, had had some influence on Danish thinking, Stalin's policy after 1945 soon reversed this. Along with the change went a stern rejection of the pacifism of the past, with the popular slogan, "Never again a ninth of April," the date when the Nazis took over Denmark in what was virtually a bloodless occupation.

In the months of uncertainty just after VE day, some form of Scandinavian cooperation—a Scandinavian bloc —was widely discussed in the three capitals. But the differences were great, particularly on the side of Norway, where the ties with Britain and the Allies through the government-in-exile in London had been so strong. In the fall of 1948, Sweden came forward with a proposal for a Scandinavian defense union made up of the three powers on the Scandinavian peninsula. Such a union would have no connection with either East or West. Denmark was more inclined to agree to a Nordic union even though under the Swedish proposal Greenland, the Danish province in the northern hemisphere, would be excluded. The Danes said finally they would go along with whatever conclusion was reached by Sweden and Norway. Influenced by the need to modernize its army, with help from the United States, Norway ruled out the Swedish proposal.

With this, Norway and Denmark entered the final negotiations for participation in the North Atlantic alliance. While there has been no doubt of their loyalty to NATO, they made certain reservations to their membership. No NATO bases were to be established on Danish or

Norwegian soil. In the first instance this was a disappointment, since tentative plans had called for an extensive NATO air base in Denmark, with its proximity to the Soviet Union. The reservation was particularly important for Norway in light of its border of about 150 miles with the Soviet Union in the far north. Then when tactical nuclear weapons became such a major part of NATO strategy both nations ruled out putting any tactical nukes within their respective borders.

The idea of a Scandanivian defense bloc had been strongly denounced by the Soviets. When it became known that Norway intended to join NATO, Moscow delivered a stern warning against such a step, at the same time making representations to determine whether the Norwegians would make air and naval bases available to its allies. The Norwegian government gave the following reply, which has been the foundation of Norwegian policy:

Norway will never be a party to a policy with aggressive intentions. It will never permit Norwegian territory to be used in the service of a policy of this kind. The Norwegian government will not be party to any agreement with other states involving obligations on the part of Norway to make available for the armed forces of foreign powers bases on Norwegian territory as long as Norway is not attacked or subject to the threat of attack.

With the exception of Turkey, the only other NATO country with a border with the Soviet Union, Norway in the far north is perhaps the most sensitive point in the NATO defense line. A major part of the Soviet nuclear ballistic missile submarine force is built and based in the Kola peninsula area, close to Norway's northern border. The Kolafjord and the Murmansk area have the only ice-free harbor facilities in the European part of the Soviet Union. An ever increasing share of the Soviet naval buildup takes place within the northern fleet on Norway's bleak, cold doorstep, with its sparse population. About

$1.726 billion in military aid from the United States and Canada went into the construction of Norwegian airfields, naval bases, radar stations, and for modern weapons systems for land, naval, and air forces. Espionage and the threat and actuality of overflights have been a constant source of friction in the north.

Sweden was alone. It would be hard to exaggerate the pressures put on the Swedes both before and after the ratification of the NATO alliance. The main objective of the American embassy in Stockholm was to close the gap in the Nordic defense line with the incorporation of Sweden in the alliance. One reason the Swedes gave for resisting these pressures was consideration for Finland, compelled to live in an uneasy peace with the superpower to the east. The Finns tended to resent this reasoning, convinced that they could take care of themselves.

President Urho Kekkonen was proving as a skilled tactician that it was possible to live side by side with the Soviet Union and still maintain a considerable measure of independence. In 1948 a twenty-year pact of friendship, cooperation, and mutual assistance was signed with Moscow. This was later extended to 1990. Whenever trouble threatens, Kekkonen flies to the Soviet Union to talk with Leonid Brezhnev and others in the Politburo. A large, impressive man, he has developed over the years a remarkable face-to-face relationship with the men of power in the Kremlin.

The pressures applied to Sweden at that time were not without a response in the country. The fiery editor of *Dagens Nyheter*, Herbert Tingsten, was an ardent proponent of Sweden's participation in NATO. And there were others of influence believing that after what had happened in the Second World War, neutrality for one country depending on its own resources and its own defense was impossible. One argument was that neutrality was a betrayal of Norway and Denmark and the ordeal they had endured after 1940. Moreover, with Sweden out, the deterrent

force of NATO in the north was weakened and the danger of aggressive action by the Soviet Union enhanced.

The conviction of neutrality was embedded above all in the Social Democratic party. These were the heirs of the men and women who had labored in the fields and forests, conditioned by an isolation that was in part geography, in part a self-sufficiency grown out of the soil and the communal life of the church. But the Social Democrats were also acutely aware of trends in the world and the threat of a severe depression after 1945 such as had occurred at the end of the First World War.

As we have seen, the ideologues in the left of the party had come forward shortly after the war with a 27-point plan for nationalization of the means of production in a planned economy. But as the fears of a depression vanished and prosperity returned, with foreign order books filled and overfilled, the proposed planned economy lost support. Once again the private sector, the unions, and the government worked together to promote the level of productivity and the standard of living. This was the condition of compromise that would, or so it seemed, go on into an indefinite future. One of the chief architects of a planned economy had been Gunnar Myrdal, minister of commerce in the Social Democratic government from 1945 to 1947 and executive director of the Wigforss commission. With the abandonment of the commission's proposed program, Myrdal turned his attention thereafter to foreign policy.

Gunnar and his wife, Alva, are two of the most remarkable figures in Swedish life, their influence extending far beyond the borders of their own country. To see them as I did in 1978 in their spacious apartment in Stockholm's Old Town is like seeing two romantic characters out of an historic play. Alva at seventy-six, still suffering from the aftermath of a severe heart attack, and Gunnar at seventy-nine with some evidence of the consequences of a motor accident years ago in Geneva, were

planning a semester of lectures and seminars at the University of Wisconsin, to be followed by a similar academic regimen at the University of Texas. They were both so full of enthusiasm and anecdotes of past and present that a visitor felt that his role must be that of umpire to parcel out the time between them.

This remarkable pair had perhaps more to do with the direction of Swedish foreign policy in the postwar years than any other individuals. They shaped it above all through their active participation in myriad ways in the United Nations and with the Third World. Early in her career Alva Myrdal was involved with the social and economic agencies of the U.N., becoming director of the social sciences for UNESCO. In 1950 she was named Swedish ambassador to India and minister to Sri Lanka, Burma, and Nepal. An intensive exposure for nearly six years to the immediacy of poverty, hunger, and population explosion confirmed her already strong interest in the developing nations and brought into focus for her the contrast between the rich industrialized world of the West, of which Sweden was a prime example, and the three-fourths of the world's population eking out a bare existence.

It was, however, her appointment as chief of the Swedish delegation to the eighteen-nation disarmament conference at Geneva that gave a new center to her interests. With some interruptions she served as a delegate to that conference for twelve years. Repeatedly she sided with the Third World representatives in opposition to the two superpowers on the broad issues of disarmament. As the futile debate continued, the experience for this idealistic woman, steeped in the conviction of neutrality and the reforms of the welfare state, was often frustrating and even embittering.

Her long disillusionment was put in cumulative form in her book *The Game of Disarmament*. Drawing not only on her own experience but on the studies of the Swedish

International Peace Research Institute (SIPRI), she condemned the spiraling arms race, with its never ending search for new and more lethal weapons. The results of the SALT I agreement abolishing the antiballistic missile and putting a ceiling on the numbers of offensive weapons she dismissed as inconsequential, since the mountain of instruments of mass destruction—weapons is hardly an adequate word—continued to grow on each side of the great divide. The way in which she assigned equal blame to the two superpowers offended Americans who had struggled with the effort in an open society to bring about mutual disarmament.

A measure of the important part she has played in shaping Swedish foreign policy was her selection as chairman of the government committee that formulated the constitution and plan of work of SIPRI. Gunnar Myrdal became chairman of SIPRI's international board until they both left Sweden for two years in 1973. SIPRI has through its internationally recruited staff scrupulously kept its independence, according to Mrs. Myrdal. This is assured by the fact that it is entirely financed on the Swedish national budget, working under stringent legal rules about non-interference by any authorities in its activities, including the selection of research projects. SIPRI, commemorating in its founding Sweden's 150 years of peace, has had a great influence on public opinion not only in Sweden but abroad.

In the early sixties, some argued for nuclear arms for Sweden. As a member of the parliamentary Defense Planning Commission, Mrs. Myrdal became one of the strongest opponents of a Swedish nuclear force, even though some members of her own party favored it. Her position was strengthened when she became a member of the cabinet in 1966. In 1968 Sweden formally and unilaterally renounced nuclear weapons and soon thereafter all chemical and biological weapons.

With regard to the ratification of the 1925 protocol barring the use of chemical weapons, Mrs. Myrdal describes a dramatic encounter with the United States delegation at the U.N. in New York. A luxurious luncheon was given in her honor and she was then, in her words, stood up against the wall, and the following question regarding ratification of the protocol on chemical and biological weapons was put to her: "Are you sincere in saying that nonratification is preferable to ratification where we make reservations so as to get the nonlethal weapons exempted." Her response was a firm yes. As she was aware, chemical weapons were then being used in the Vietnam war. Along with the faded hope of a worldwide disarmament conference to be convoked by the U.N. General Assembly, she recounts many painful disappointments:

" The truly astonishing fact is that people all over the world have become conditioned to live on unconcerned about the steadily increasing risk that nuclear holocaust might suddenly destroy us all and our civilization. Only in Japan has a lasting anxiety persisted, rekindled time and again by "Hiroshima anniversaries." Otherwise postwar history has only for brief periods and in a few countries witnessed some perturbations of the public calm. A groundswell was caused after the Bikini megaton blast in 1954 hit the Japanese fishing boat *Lucky Dragon* with radioactive debris. Prominent scientists mounted a protest movement against the atom bomb, especially in Britain, where it was unsuccessful, and in Sweden where it scored success. . . .

The lack of concern is the result not only of our opportunistic inclination to turn our attention away from disagreeable thoughts, but also of reckless and systematic propaganda by the vested interests and their obedient servants among politicians, governments, military and foreign policy bureaucracies, and even captive scientists. The mass media serve as megaphones for this propaganda while blacking out our knowledge of facts and rational reasoning.

The Second World War had convinced many Swedes that the major powers were ruthless, without scruples of any kind, driven simply by a desire for conquest, with the possible exception of America. Nowhere, not even in the fiercest antiwar centers in the United States, was feeling against the American action in Vietnam stronger than in Sweden. One reason was the presence of several hundred—the exact number was never established —American deserters and draft dodgers. But even without their participation, and apparently at times incitation, the protest in the form of repeated demonstrations would have occurred. Swedish newspapers and the Swedish state-owned television and radio gave the war thorough coverage. In the Swedish view, here was a great power, a superpower, using the most lethal of modern techniques, short of nuclear weapons, to subdue a small Asian country resisting the American invasion with comparatively little help from any source. The television screen brought into every living room scenes of the havoc wreaked on civilians and their villages. As American bombing grew in intensity, so did the anger of those who felt deeply the injustice of this far-off war. The issue united virtually every political faction from extreme left to right. It became a love-hate relationship, for what Swede could forget the great reservoir of Swedish Americans in the new country, many in positions of importance both in the private and public sectors, even as American bombs were falling on Hanoi.

The archetype of this relationship is Gunnar Myrdal, who has had such close ties with the United States while at the same time taking a conspicuous part in the Vietnam protest. He participated in various protest demonstrations in Stockholm, and he was president of the non-governmental International Commission on U.S. War Crimes in Indochina that held extended hearings in Oslo, Stockholm, and Copenhagen. Myrdal was one of two principal speakers at a rally that filled Madison Square Garden. As he was to complain in the aftermath of Vietnam,

the American press paid scant attention to his strictures on the unwinnable war whether he spoke in Stockholm or New York. Let it be added that modesty and self-efface-ment are not part of his temperament.

Myrdal had every reason to understand America. Be-tween 1938 and 1942 he spent virtually all his time in a study that took him throughout the country for the back-ground of his two-volume work *An American Dilemma: The Negro Problem and Democracy*, which was published in 1944. In commissioning and financing the study the Carnegie Corporation had chosen Myrdal as a leading political econ-omist from a country with virtually no racial problem what-soever. The Carnegie trustees had called on him for "a comprehensive study of the Negro in the United States to be undertaken in a wholly objective way as a social phe-nomenon." Beginning his study with a conviction of the "American Creed" as it embodied liberty, equality, justice, and the rule of law and not men he reached, as he was to say in a lecture given in 1974 at City College in New York, the belief that constructive change was almost certain to occur. He predicted the "black revolt" that was to be the chief instrument in a profound reordering of relations be-tween the races. His lecture in New York was a preface to writing *An American Dilemma Revisited*. This recorded the changes of thirty years following the original study, which had been widely hailed as a landmark in analyzing the sta-tus of the two races.

With the Swedish reaction to the Vietnam war growing in intensity, President Richard Nixon sent a black educator as ambassador to Stockholm. Jerome H. Holland, serious, dedicated to the education of his people, was pres-ident of Hampton Institute at Hampton, Virginia. He had had no diplomatic experience and little or no firsthand knowledge of the politics of Sweden and northern Europe. On his arrival in February 1968, he was greeted by a demonstration consisting mostly of the young shouting and waving placards. From the crowd, as the demonstra-

tion went on, rose the shout, "House nigger." This was a
shock to a people who had considered themselves free
of racial prejudice. It was said the insult had come from
one of the American deserters, although this was never
established.

Under a great handicap, Holland proved a hard-
working and able ambassador. He acquired enough Swedish to make brief simple speeches in his travels around the
country. But the odds against him were too heavy. Opinion in both America and Sweden had been aroused when
Olof Palme joined a demonstration in which the North
Vietnamese ambassador to Moscow took part on February
21, 1968. Palme was then minister of education, a leader in
the Social Democratic party, and close adviser to the then
prime minister, Tage Erlander. A brilliant intellectual,
Palme was to become head of the government a year later,
in 1969. In language that might have been heard on any
American campus, Palme addressed the demonstrators at-
tacking both France, for having tried to resume control
over Indochina, and the United States, for the war in
Vietnam:

These events give us a feeling of agitation, sympathy,
despair. But feelings can quickly flare up and equally
quickly disappear if they do not find a hold in a cause or a
context. We should therefore be aware that these suffer-
ings of individuals are the bitter logical consequence of an
erroneous and deeply unjustified policy conducted over
the past 20 years. . . .

In spite of the enormous military contribution, things
are going badly, presumably worse and worse, for the
United States in Vietnam. The whole world therefore
trembles at the thought of the next step. The questions are
put in fear: Shall it be nuclear weapons? Who then will remain to liberate? And would this not mean that a third
world war is a fact? Shall the blow be directed against the
dams of the Red River? It would be a terrible annihilation
of human beings.

He directed his attack, too, at the regime in Saigon as corrupt, inefficient, indifferent to social demands, unable to survive without the 500,000 American troops in Vietnam. Observing that the National Liberation Front in the north had little chance because of the war to demonstrate what its policy would mean, he recommended a study of the front's programs, which would command a wide coalition once victory had been won. "The domestic policy program could be accepted on the whole by the political parties in Sweden," Palme said.

The climax was at Christmas 1972, when Palme as prime minister made a statement comparing the bombing of Cambodia to the genocide practiced by the Nazis. This infuriated Nixon, particularly since it coincided with the demonstrations on campuses across the country in America by students and teachers angered at the destruction of that once lovely country. The end was clearly in sight. It was not long before Holland came home, ostensibly for consultations but not to return. The Swedish ambassador in Washington, Hubert de Beche, who had begun his tour of duty in 1964, found doors increasingly closed to him, and he left in 1974.

This was the beginning of a painful breach in what had been close and friendly relations between the two countries. Fortunately De Beche's second in command remained as chargé d'affaire. Leif Leifland is one of the outstanding figures in a foreign service noted for its high level of training and skill. Despite the inaccessibility of top officials in the administration, Leifland carried on with quiet dignity, doing all he could to prevent the breach from becoming too damaging. In 1975 Sweden sent to Washington a three-star ambassador, Count Wilhelm Wachtmeister, who had held an important position in the Foreign Office. With his charming wife, Ulla, he soon made a wide circle of friends, and the threads of a happier past were knit together again. Two years after his return to Stockholm, Leifland was made secretary general of the

foreign service, jumped over the heads of many seniors to a position of great responsibility.

A strong left-wing bent carried over from the deep feeling over the Vietnam war. This found expression when Secretary of State Henry Kissinger visited Stockholm at the invitation of the government on May 23, 1976. He was greeted by a massive demonstration that equaled or exceeded those that had gone on at the peak of American involvement in the war in Indochina. This was more remarkable in that intensity of feeling in the United States had subsided. An editorial in *Dagens Nyheter* before his arrival stressed that while his star was declining he was nevertheless one of the most influential men in the world and Sweden should welcome an opportunity to hear his views.

On his arrival at Arlandea airport Kissinger made a conciliatory statement. He said that the relationship between the two countries had been better in recent years even though "we do not have the same opinions. . . . We understand Sweden's policy of non-interference and neutrality which results in different attitudes toward international affairs. We on our side have a feeling of responsibility for the security of free peoples and also for the democratic principles that unite our countries." On the day after his arrival he had a six-hour talk with Prime Minister Olof Palme and Foreign Minister Sven Andersson. He characterized the discussion as very useful. "I did not come here to make us agree on specific questions and we never had the intention of drawing up a balance sheet. On some questions we agree, on others not."

They talked about Africa, the relationship between East and West, and the possiblity of large-scale communist influence in southern Europe. This was just before the Italian elections, when it was predicted that the Communist party would make sizable gains and perhaps even attain a majority. Kissinger, as he was to do later when he spoke to a meeting of the Swedish Foreign Policy Institute, stressed that the American position toward any Western

European nation that had a powerful, if not a dominant, communist element would be certain to shift. He told Palme that it was useful to exchange information with a neutral nation like Sweden because of Sweden's closeness to Third World and neutral countries of which the United States had only a limited knowledge. The stress in their talk was that no sharp antagonism existed between their respective countries.

As he said on his arrival, Kissinger had been forewarned that there would be demonstrations against him, and he was not disappointed. On his first day in Sweden an estimated 13,000 demonstrators marched, perhaps the largest demonstration that had occurred in Sweden since the start of the Vietnam war. As the demonstrators advanced toward the American embassy they shouted "Kissinger murderer," "USA out of Korea," "Stop the USA Imperialism." More than fifty different organizations speaking for Chile, Uruguay, Cuba, Turkey, Korea, and the African countries were represented. They were united in their attack on American policy, with Kissinger as the embodiment of that policy. One large sign held by a half-dozen demonstrators read "Condemn the war criminal—send Kissinger away." Helmeted policemen ringed the embassy.

The demonstration was a striking enactment of the role of Sweden in a troubled world. Here were the young who had escaped from repression and fear in their respective countries. They had jobs, or if they were newcomers they were occupied with encouraging the spirit of dissent: writing, preaching, helping more of their fellow countrymen to try to flee the bonds of oppression. They had been spurred on by Vietnam and the intensity of the Swedish attack on the American war in that small country. Sweden was a safe haven for the oppressed from the four corners of the earth, and in pouring out into the streets they could put the blame on the American who had presided over American foreign policy.

In his speech at the Foreign Policy Institute, Kissinger said, according to those who heard him, that whether anyone liked it or not Sweden, having resisted all the pleas to become part of NATO, nevertheless enjoyed shelter under the American nuclear umbrella. He was also frank to say that America's determination to support Western Europe would not be so firm should communism take over in one or more of the NATO nations. The secretary used stern language in talking about the economic failures of the communist countries to the East. He accused the Soviet Union of trying to compensate for earlier failures by launching attacks against the periphery. The reference was clearly to Angola. The United States, he said, would not tolerate such attacks. The two-day visit put American policy squarely on the line at the same time that it showed the intense feeling of the extreme left in Sweden, with so many causes having been taken over by a small minority. This might be called one of the perquisites of affluence: to bleed for the prisoners of the Chilean junta and the victims of the South Korean dictatorship.

Much as it would like to stay outside the United States' quarrels with the Soviet Union, Sweden has more than once found itself caught in the middle.

The supersonic plane, for example, was a remarkable achievement for a nation of 8,000,000. In a world bristling with armaments, Sweden with its high technology was not to be left out. But in the context of Sweden's strict neutrality and the government's high-minded criticism of the military and foreign policy of other nations the creation of a supersonic fighter plane was bound to cause complications. This is part of the paradox of a people determined to preserve the values of the past when those values are being rapidly eroded away almost everywhere else.

The plane with which Sweden's air force is equipped was developed by Saab-Scania. While it ranks in cost above advanced American and Soviet supersonic fighters and in performance is somewhat below their level, nevertheless

foreign sales seemed a possibility in order to relieve the burden of the plane, called the Viggen. Sweden's restrictions on arms sales, related to the policy of neutrality, are severe. Finally, however, a deal was made with India for purchase outright of forty Viggens and eighty to be manufactured under license in India.

The engines in the Viggen are manufactured under an American license by Volvo Flygmotor in Trollhaten, giving the U.S. a role in such a decision. To the surprise of practically everyone, including the prime minister, the deal with India was vetoed by the Carter administration in Washington. Fälldin sent Minister of Commerce Steffan Burenstam Linder to Washington to present Sweden's case to Secretary of State Cyrus Vance. But the Carter administration would not yield.

A rash of indignant editorials followed the news of Washington's veto. The real reason, it was said, was Washington's concern over the military balance between India and Pakistan and the need to offset the Swedish sale by providing India's neighbor with advanced American fighters. Why, the editorials asked, should President Carter be attempting to govern Sweden?

One of the most critical editorials appeared in the conservative *Svenska Dagbladet*. It pointed out that the United States had had no problem when it came to exporting a much more advanced plane, the F-15, to Israel and Egypt in the critical Middle East. So strict are Swedish regulations applied to this region that not even ammunition for sporting guns can be exported there. According to the editorial, Washington openly opposed Viggen when four NATO countries were interested in buying the Swedish plane. "Then it was said that they understood Sweden's need for a strong defense industry. That industry should, however, sell in other markets. But now Washington threatens with the veto."

The deal meant millions of dollars in direct sales and in license to manufacture in India. More important, it

meant work for 500 to 600 workers for several years. This was of the utmost importance for Sweden's aircraft industry and the meagerly funded defense establishment. "The truth of the matter is," the *Dagbladet* editorial concluded, "that India wants to replace old planes. Sweden cannot stop them from doing that. Some other country will get the order."

Knowing the principles that govern Swedish policy in this field, there was no reason for the United States government to act as guardian, said an editorial in the liberal newspaper *Expressen*. The only result of the veto was that French and British manufacturers would get big orders. Was this the intention? Only one newspaper, *Dagens Nyheter*, supported the Carter veto, observing that the Swedish government had been criticized in the Riksdag in the spring for lack of sufficient control over the arms trade.

With the rivalry of the two superpowers in every department, it was a new world in which neutral Sweden found itself, a world in which the rules of the past no longer prevailed. This was illustrated also by a long controversy with Washington over another proposed sale. Moscow wanted to buy a computerized air control system for a new airport being built for the 1980 Olympics. But because certain component parts were of American origin or under American license, efforts to get approval for the sale met with a prolonged bureaucratic hassle. The dispute was strung out for more than a year until final approval was granted for a contract for $60 million for the computerized system. Actually, Swedish trade with the entire East bloc is at most 5.5 percent, of which about 2 percent is with the Soviet Union, and the largest share with Poland. Trade with the United States is 6 percent of Sweden's total. And Sweden has been anything but an admirer of the Soviet system. At the time of the Soviet invasion of Czechoslovakia in 1968 opinion was strongly stirred in criticism of a brutal act against the mild dissidence of a So-

viet satellite. When defectors have taken refuge in Sweden the government has stood firm against the stern demands of Moscow. Quietly the then foreign minister, Mrs. Söder, directed an effort to try to obtain the release of the family of a Soviet sailor who deserted his ship in the Baltic.

Attitudes toward the United States continue to be mixed. Years of friendliness toward another democratic, industrious people compete today with concern over U.S. policies. Gunnar Myrdal, with his close American ties, epitomizes the Swede who admires the United States but is troubled by its behavior. Both in *An American Dilemma* and in his frequent lectures at American universities, Myrdal showed an understanding of and a sympathy for the American way of life as expounded in the highest ideals still cherished as a part of the American heritage. But this has not blunted his sharp challenge of the American posture in a troubled and deeply divided world. That challenge was one of the principal themes running through his Nobel Memorial Lecture delivered on March 17, 1975, in Stockholm following the award of the Nobel prize for economics to him the previous year. Under the title "The Equality Issue in World Development," he made frequent references to the discrepancy in providing aid to developing countries among the various industrialized nations. Speaking of the decreasing mortality rate due to cheap and powerful medical technology made available after the Second World War, he went on to say that people will continue to live and breed only to suffer debilitating conditions constantly reducing their efficiency and consequently the productivity of the labor force:

In this situation there are certainly moral and rational reasons for a new world order and, to begin with, for aid on a strikingly higher level. In particular people in the rich countries should be challenged to bring down their lavish food consumption. It is estimated that if the average American were to reduce his consumption of beef, pork,

t. The Board for Nordic Development Projects pro-
sed that joint development cooperation should be un-
rtaken in Mozambique. Sweden alone allocated $25
lion to Mozambique for the fiscal year 1979-80. It is to
carried out in collaboration with the U.N. Food and Ag-
lture Organization. To give Nordic joint efforts in de-
pment aid a firmer base, a committee of government
cials was appointed under the Nordic Council of Min-
s. The Nordic Council, a consultative assembly of par-
entarians and cabinet ministers of Sweden, Norway,
mark, Finland, and Iceland, was created in 1953. The
mittee reports to the council on development assist-
and serves, too, as a forum for informal talks on bilat-
and multilateral cooperation.

The scope of Swedish aid in Africa is extraordinary. It
des Angola, Botswana, Cape Verde, Ethiopia,
ea-Bissau, Lesotho, Somalia, Swaziland, Tunisia, and
bia. In addition Sweden supports the East African
munity and other regional activities as well as research
tions scattered through the African continent. Par-
stress is put on the situation in southern Africa, with
sed support for the free states in the area. The state-
of the aid authority of the new coalition government
e 1977-78 budget included the following: "Swedish
ll increase to liberation movements, to educational
ms for refugees, and to other forms of support to
s of apartheid and racism, extended in accordance
nited Nations resolutions." The funds allocated for
rpose, amounting to just under $10 million, would
beration movements in South Africa, Namibia, and
rn Rhodesia. Sweden also helps to finance the
a Institute in Lusaka. The largest single recipient in
s Tanzania, which got more than $50 million in the
budget. Improved water supply in rural areas is
he main goals of Swedish assistance.

Asia Swedish bilateral aid is more narrowly distrib-
wo of the countries in most desperate need,

and poultry by 10 percent 12,000,000 tons or more of
grain would be saved. This would mean making so much
more food aid possible, saving perhaps five times as many
million people as tons released, or even more, from starvation in the poorest countries. This reduction of meat consumption would be in the rational interest of the American
people itself and much less than is recommended for
health reasons by the American Heart Association: one-
third. Beyond overeating comes the colossal waste by
overserving and spoilage. To a varying and usually lesser
extent the same holds true in all developed countries.

He gave Sweden, where aid was to increase by 25 percent a year, a high mark. Having been critical of the United
States and most other developed countries for giving aid
with the justification of self-interest, he added that a "nationalistic motive" could never with any credibility be
presented to the Swedish people. The other Scandinavian
countries, the Netherlands, and Canada were also given
credit for the extent of their aid and the motives behind it.

Myrdal, who for ten years was executive secretary of
the United Nations Economic Commission for Europe,
took a gloomy view of the future of the U.N. He felt that
the two superpowers had used it for their own purposes.
They had ignored the resolutions of the General Assembly
whenever they chose to. The veto built into the Security
Council had insured big-power domination. The collateral
agencies such as the development fund were falling far
short of their goals for lack of funds that could come only
from the rich industrialized nations.

As one rich industrialized nation, Sweden has certainly given stout support to the United Nations. In a practical way Sweden has contributed to the U.N. in four crises
that threatened war. Swedish forces were contributed for
peacekeeping operations in the Congo, in Cyprus, more
than once in the Middle East. Despite a continuing strong
stand of nonalignment, Sweden was a charter member

gloomy view of U.N.

of the European Free Trade Association. While flirting briefly with membership in the European Economic Community, the government in 1971 ruled this out as contrary to neutrality. Two years later an arrangement was agreed to giving Sweden a free trade deal with the EEC. Sweden also plays an active role in the Organization for Economic Cooperation and Development, the Council of Europe, and GATT (General Agreement on Tariffs and Trade). Sweden in 1975 became a member of the International Energy Agency formed under OECD auspices to try to evolve a common Western response to the challenge of quadrupled OPEC oil prices. As an active member of the International Atomic Energy Agency, the coalition government had a forum for expressing concern over the ever expanding development of nuclear power reactors and the grave potential dangers of such an involvement.

In its participation in international programs to improve the lot of people in Third World countries, Sweden has set a record few other nations can match. It has undertaken to keep its contribution to the U.N. multinational organizations and to bilateral foreign aid at 1 percent of the country's gross national product. It is the only country that has attained this level. The United States in 1975 contributed .27 percent of GNP, Switzerland .19, Germany .40. The figure for the Netherlands was .75, for Norway .66. Even when, under the new coalition government, borrowing abroad became necessary to meet budgetary deficits, the goal of increasing foreign assistance by 25 percent a year was maintained. This meant that the total of foreign aid was roughly equivalent to the $2 billion borrowed abroad in 1977. Sweden is one of the largest contributors to the United Nations Development Program and the United Nation International Children's Fund. Food aid, tied to various international food programs with Swedish contributions in kind, amounts to close to $150 million in value.

Of the twenty-two countri[es]
bilateral aid from Sweden, by f[ar]
to reunited Vietnam. The total
1977-78 was nearly $100 milli[on]
$6 million over the previous fi[ve]
the aid was for a paper and
which will, it is hoped, go fo[r]
children. But Sweden discove[red]
the problems inherent in the
trialized country with a hig[h]
war-ravaged Vietnam. At a
session at the National Pres[s]
Minister Ullsten was asked
Cambodia would make a d[...]
He replied that the whole
struction of the pulp and
with the Johnson group, o[ne]
aggregations with extensi[ve]
thanks to cost overruns, th[e]
is the difficulty of findi[ng]
workers for the technical
testing. In the initial stag[e]
and pulp manufacture w[...]
investment in the Vie[tnam]
housing, schools, medic[al]
addition Sweden is pr[...]
general hospital. This
massive damage done

One interesting de[...]
between the Nordic
The joint stand they h[...]
other multilateral bod[ies]
jectives they share in
Nordic development
jointly financed wit[h]
Tanzania this joint ai[d]

Bangladesh and Laos, are beneficiaries, with the former receiving $25 million, the latter $9 million in the 1977-78 budget. India got the largest amount, $60 million, Sri Lanka $17 million, Pakistan $7 million. Out of the bilateral total, another approximately $200 million went for disaster relief, special programs, humanitarian aid to Latin America and voluntary organizations. The only country for which aid was reduced in the 1977-78 budget was Cuba, cut from $10 million to $8 million.

The Swedish aid program is notable for the thoroughness with which it is planned. Commitments are made for a three-year period after extensive consultation with representatives of the recipient countries. This is in conspicuous contrast with larger powers with a far greater aid potential that too often follow a slapdash, improvised, off-again-on-again kind of programming.

As with all cabinet ministries, the guidelines are set at the top, in this instance by Ola Ullsten, then minister for international development cooperation, within the Ministry for Foreign Affairs. Later to become deputy prime minister as well as to continue to hold the aid post, he was responsible for the aid program, assisted by the Office for International Development Cooperation. But the minister is not burdened by a large bureaucracy. The task of initiating and vetting programs and seeing that they are carried out falls to the Swedish International Development Authority (SIDA). On the basis of SIDA's proposals the government draws up instructions for the annual consultations covering the volume and nature of Swedish aid during the fiscal year to come. Indicative planning figures for the two following years are also presented. The Swedish government concludes an agreement with all program countries on terms and procedures for the transfer of resources, including procurement rules and terms and procedures for the provision of personnel. In Swedish embassies in almost every recipient country an aide is assigned to work with the local development authority. Since 1974

Sweden has concluded agreements on economic, industrial, and technical cooperation with countries which are
not among the principal recipients of Swedish aid, for example, Algeria, Egypt, Iraq, Iran, and Libya. Cooperation
with Algeria has been facilitated by the fact that it has been
possible to utilize aid to help finance certain investments
in the field of vocational education in connection with industrial projects being carried out by Swedish corporations.

"I consider it important," Ullsten said in presenting
his budget, "that we retain the possibility of using to some
extent assistance funds for financing broader cooperation
through consultants, authorities, and corporations in countries where our assistance is being gradually wound up as
well as in other developing countries."

In his introductory statement Ullsten faced the fact
that the poorer developing countries without oil resources
and only a limited potential for export of raw materials
were being forced to meet their capital requirements by
short-term commercial borrowing. This has meant, he
noted, that the already grave debt problems of certain developing countries have grown still more serious. Interest
payments and amortization—debt servicing—are increasing at an even faster rate as these developing countries
have to borrow more and more on the open market where
interest rates are higher and credit periods shorter than for
assistance credits. This means that an ever increasing share
of export revenues has to go for repaying old loans. In
1975 debt servicing for the non–oil-producing developing
countries was 11.7 percent of the value of exports as
against 8.3 percent the year before.

It is understandable that Sweden, caught in somewhat
the same vice of deficits and commercial loans unprecedented in the nation's recent history, should have been so
aware of the ominous meaning of the ever increasing ratio
of poverty to debt in the peoples of the developing lands
without energy resources. The larger powers, with far

and poultry by 10 percent 12,000,000 tons or more of grain would be saved. This would mean making so much more food aid possible, saving perhaps five times as many million people as tons released, or even more, from starvation in the poorest countries. This reduction of meat consumption would be in the rational interest of the American people itself and much less than is recommended for health reasons by the American Heart Association: one-third. Beyond overeating comes the colossal waste by overserving and spoilage. To a varying and usually lesser extent the same holds true in all developed countries.

He gave Sweden, where aid was to increase by 25 percent a year, a high mark. Having been critical of the United States and most other developed countries for giving aid with the justification of self-interest, he added that a "nationalistic motive" could never with any credibility be presented to the Swedish people. The other Scandinavian countries, the Netherlands, and Canada were also given credit for the extent of their aid and the motives behind it.

Myrdal, who for ten years was executive secretary of the United Nations Economic Commission for Europe, took a gloomy view of the future of the U.N. He felt that the two superpowers had used it for their own purposes. They had ignored the resolutions of the General Assembly whenever they chose to. The veto built into the Security Council had insured big-power domination. The collateral agencies such as the development fund were falling far short of their goals for lack of funds that could come only from the rich industrialized nations.

As one rich industrialized nation, Sweden has certainly given stout support to the United Nations. In a practical way Sweden has contributed to the U.N. in four crises that threatened war. Swedish forces were contributed for peacekeeping operations in the Congo, in Cyprus, more than once in the Middle East. Despite a continuing strong stand of nonalignment, Sweden was a charter member

of the European Free Trade Association. While flirting briefly with membership in the European Economic Community, the government in 1971 ruled this out as contrary to neutrality. Two years later an arrangement was agreed to giving Sweden a free trade deal with the EEC. Sweden also plays an active role in the Organization for Economic Cooperation and Development, the Council of Europe, and GATT (General Agreement on Tariffs and Trade). Sweden in 1975 became a member of the International Energy Agency formed under OECD auspices to try to evolve a common Western response to the challenge of quadrupled OPEC oil prices. As an active member of the International Atomic Energy Agency, the coalition government had a forum for expressing concern over the ever expanding development of nuclear power reactors and the grave potential dangers of such an involvement.

In its participation in international programs to improve the lot of people in Third World countries, Sweden has set a record few other nations can match. It has undertaken to keep its contribution to the U.N. multinational organizations and to bilateral foreign aid at 1 percent of the country's gross national product. It is the only country that has attained this level. The United States in 1975 contributed .27 percent of GNP, Switzerland .19, Germany .40. The figure for the Netherlands was .75, for Norway .66. Even when, under the new coalition government, borrowing abroad became necessary to meet budgetary deficits, the goal of increasing foreign assistance by 25 percent a year was maintained. This meant that the total of foreign aid was roughly equivalent to the $2 billion borrowed abroad in 1977. Sweden is one of the largest contributors to the United Nations Development Program and the United Nation International Children's Fund. Food aid, tied to various international food programs with Swedish contributions in kind, amounts to close to $150 million in value.

Of the twenty-two countries that receive emergency bilateral aid from Sweden, by far the largest amount goes to reunited Vietnam. The total allocated for the fiscal year 1977-78 was nearly $100 million. This was an addition of $6 million over the previous fiscal year. The largest part of the aid was for a paper and pulp factory, the output of which will, it is hoped, go for textbooks for Vietnamese children. But Sweden discovered in organizing this project the problems inherent in the difference between an industrialized country with a high technology and primitive, war-ravaged Vietnam. At a recent question-and-answer session at the National Press Club in Washington, Prime Minister Ullsten was asked whether Vietnam's invasion of Cambodia would make a difference in this annual grant. He replied that the whole matter was under study. Construction of the pulp and paper plant was contracted for with the Johnson group, one of Sweden's largest industrial aggregations with extensive overseas business. Already, thanks to cost overruns, the price has doubled. One reason is the difficulty of finding sufficient skilled Vietnamese workers for the technical tasks of machine installation and testing. In the initial stages at least, raw material for paper and pulp manufacture will have to be imported. Swedish investment in the Vietnamese infrastructure includes housing, schools, medical centers, roads, and railroads. In addition Sweden is providing a children's hospital and a general hospital. This is all seen as repairing in part the massive damage done by American bombing.

One interesting development is the close cooperation between the Nordic nations in development assistance. The joint stand they have often taken in the U.N. and in other multilateral bodies gives increased weight to the objectives they share in aid to the less developed countries. Nordic development projects in Tanzania and Kenya are jointly financed with the aid given to cooperatives. In Tanzania this joint aid includes an agricultural training pro-

ject. The Board for Nordic Development Projects proposed that joint development cooperation should be undertaken in Mozambique. Sweden alone allocated $25
million to Mozambique for the fiscal year 1979-80. It is to
be carried out in collaboration with the U.N. Food and Agriculture Organization. To give Nordic joint efforts in development aid a firmer base, a committee of government
officials was appointed under the Nordic Council of Ministers. The Nordic Council, a consultative assembly of par-
liamentarians and cabinet ministers of Sweden, Norway,
Denmark, Finland, and Iceland, was created in 1953. The
committee reports to the council on development assistance and serves, too, as a forum for informal talks on bilateral and multilateral cooperation.

The scope of Swedish aid in Africa is extraordinary. It
includes Angola, Botswana, Cape Verde, Ethiopia,
Guinea-Bissau, Lesotho, Somalia, Swaziland, Tunisia, and
Zambia. In addition Sweden supports the East African
Community and other regional activities as well as research
institutions scattered through the African continent. Particular stress is put on the situation in southern Africa, with
increased support for the free states in the area. The statement of the aid authority of the new coalition government
on the 1977-78 budget included the following: "Swedish
aid will increase to liberation movements, to educational
programs for refugees, and to other forms of support to
victims of apartheid and racism, extended in accordance
with United Nations resolutions." The funds allocated for
that purpose, amounting to just under $10 million, would
go to liberation movements in South Africa, Namibia, and
Southern Rhodesia. Sweden also helps to finance the
Namibia Institute in Lusaka. The largest single recipient in
Africa is Tanzania, which got more than $50 million in the
1977-78 budget. Improved water supply in rural areas is
one of the main goals of Swedish assistance.

In Asia Swedish bilateral aid is more narrowly distributed. Two of the countries in most desperate need,

Bangladesh and Laos, are beneficiaries, with the former receiving $25 million, the latter $9 million in the 1977-78 budget. India got the largest amount, $60 million, Sri Lanka $17 million, Pakistan $7 million. Out of the bilateral total, another approximately $200 million went for disaster relief, special programs, humanitarian aid to Latin America and voluntary organizations. The only country for which aid was reduced in the 1977-78 budget was Cuba, cut from $10 million to $8 million.

The Swedish aid program is notable for the thoroughness with which it is planned. Commitments are made for a three-year period after extensive consultation with representatives of the recipient countries. This is in conspicuous contrast with larger powers with a far greater aid potential that too often follow a slapdash, improvised, off-again-on-again kind of programming.

As with all cabinet ministries, the guidelines are set at the top, in this instance by Ola Ullsten, then minister for international development cooperation, within the Ministry for Foreign Affairs. Later to become deputy prime minister as well as to continue to hold the aid post, he was responsible for the aid program, assisted by the Office for International Development Cooperation. But the minister is not burdened by a large bureaucracy. The task of initiating and vetting programs and seeing that they are carried out falls to the Swedish International Development Authority (SIDA). On the basis of SIDA's proposals the government draws up instructions for the annual consultations covering the volume and nature of Swedish aid during the fiscal year to come. Indicative planning figures for the two following years are also presented. The Swedish government concludes an agreement with all program countries on terms and procedures for the transfer of resources, including procurement rules and terms and procedures for the provision of personnel. In Swedish embassies in almost every recipient country an aide is assigned to work with the local development authority. Since 1974

Sweden has concluded agreements on economic, indus-trial, and technical cooperation with countries which are not among the principal recipients of Swedish aid, for example, Algeria, Egypt, Iraq, Iran, and Libya. Cooperation with Algeria has been facilitated by the fact that it has been possible to utilize aid to help finance certain investments in the field of vocational education in connection with industrial projects being carried out by Swedish corporations.

"I consider it important," Ullsten said in presenting his budget, "that we retain the possibility of using to some extent assistance funds for financing broader cooperation through consultants, authorities, and corporations in countries where our assistance is being gradually wound up as well as in other developing countries."

In his introductory statement Ullsten faced the fact that the poorer developing countries without oil resources and only a limited potential for export of raw materials were being forced to meet their capital requirements by short-term commercial borrowing. This has meant, he noted, that the already grave debt problems of certain developing countries have grown still more serious. Interest payments and amortization—debt servicing—are increasing at an even faster rate as these developing countries have to borrow more and more on the open market where interest rates are higher and credit periods shorter than for assistance credits. This means that an ever increasing share of export revenues has to go for repaying old loans. In 1975 debt servicing for the non–oil-producing developing countries was 11.7 percent of the value of exports as against 8.3 percent the year before.

It is understandable that Sweden, caught in somewhat the same vice of deficits and commercial loans unprecedented in the nation's recent history, should have been so aware of the ominous meaning of the ever increasing ratio of poverty to debt in the peoples of the developing lands without energy resources. The larger powers, with far

more reason to face the grim truth since their banks were making the commercial loans, often in excessive volume, preferred to ignore the catastrophe that could result from a breakdown of all order in the roughly half of the world's population living so close to the line of hunger. At the same time, of course, the Swedish government was thoroughly aware that its contribution, generous in proportion to its gross national product, was far too small to have any appreciable influence in altering the swift downward course of events.

In an appearance before the Second Committee of the United Nations General Assembly, Ullsten suited action to the word. He announced that Sweden was canceling more than $200 million in debts owed by eight of the world's poorest nations. He said in his speech that Sweden was taking this step in the hope that the example would be followed by others. If all developed countries should cancel debts to the poorest, it would mean an increase of nearly 20 percent in aid to those countries. For the rich, according to Ullsten, it would mean forgoing a mere .02 percent of their gross national product. The Swedish announcement followed by a month the statement of Deputy Prime Minister Arthur J. MacEachen that Canada was in the process of canceling $254 million in debts owed by the poorest of the developing nations.

Sharing the concern of many observers and responsible officials in the United States, Ullsten cited the estimated $100 billion of current account deficit in the non–oil-producing countries as a serious threat to stability. The poorest debtor countries were sagging under the effort to service debts, with 15 percent of their meager export receipts used for this purpose. With no relief for the impoverished one-third to one-half of the world's population, the threat of breakdown and even widespread revolt could not be discounted.

The Swedish foreign aid administrator spoke of the dilemma of Robert McNamara, president of the World

Bank, when he was faced with action by the U.S. House of Representatives proscribing the use of any American funds by international agencies to seven nations. One was Vietnam, recipient of by far the largest share of Swedish aid. Although the Senate later rejected the House amendment, which was eliminated from the bill as finally passed, President Carter found it necessary to issue a statement that he would use his influence to block help for the seven proscribed nations. Ullsten also referred to the fact that the United States, the largest donor, had failed at that point to come up with the fifth replenishment for the International Development Association on which the poorest nations rely for "soft" loans. Noting that the world was spending $350 billion a year on armaments and only about half a tenth of that sum on development, he called on the few rich nations now charting the course of events to share their power with the many that are only dependents.

"There is a lack of political determination and there is a lack of international mechanism," he told the U.N. General Assembly. "There is need to focus attention on concrete issues and to foster with the U.N. an understanding of our common interests as equal partners. My country pledges its firm support to such efforts."

If it was not clear before, it was clear now that Sweden was on the side of the Third World. The new right-of-center government and the budgetary deficits growing out of Sweden's own economic dilemma had made no difference in the commitment.

Swedish assistance to the Third World comes from private sources as well as government. The idealism of the cooperative movement is manifest in a larger context than the self-serving needs of consumers in Scandinavia. Initiating help for cooperatives beginning to take hold in Third World countries, it is propagandizing for the need to close the gap between the have and have-not nations. Support for cooperation in newly developing countries began in 1954 at a congress of the International Cooperative

Alliance in Paris, where a fund drive was launched with $20,000 from British cooperators as a base.

The real impetus came, however, at the Congress of the Cooperative Alliance in Stockholm in 1957. In connection with that congress, Swedish cooperators prepared an impressive exhibit on the theme "World without Boundaries." Both the need for massive aid to developing countries and support for self-help enterprises were stressed, with prominent artists enlisted to dramatize the global and domestic concerns of the cooperative spirit. The exhibit attracted 145,000 visitors and extensive comment in the press and on television. In connection with the conference, Swedish cooperators adopted the symbol for infinity, the horizontal figure eight, as their mark of identity, and it is now seen over hundreds of enterprises throughout the country.

The next stage was the start of a fund-raising campaign asking individual members to give a small contribution from their purchase dividends. Initial gifts from KF, the Cooperative Women's Guild, and Folksam, the insurance society, were a beginning. There had been some doubts as to whether individuals would contribute to a movement so removed from the immediate practical goals that had brought a far-flung organization into being. But these doubts were soon dispelled. In recent years voluntary contributions of $750,000 annually have come from consumers', oil, and farmers' cooperative societies.

The interest that grew out of the exhibit in 1957 resulted in the formation of the Swedish Cooperative Center, which took over from KF and the annual fund raising and administration of the voluntary technical assistance program made possible by these funds. Cooperating with the International Cooperative Alliance, after a conference in Kuala Lumpur, the Swedish Center decided on a center for cooperative education in Southeast Asia. Given the strength of the Indian cooperative movement and the strategic geographical location, New Delhi was chosen as the

site. Bertil Mathsson, a leading Swedish cooperator in the international field, went to New Delhi to help in organizing the educational activities of the center, including an extensive library on cooperation. Prime Minister Jawaharlal Nehru spoke at the inauguration and called for India to be "convulsed" by cooperation, a quotation used again and again throughout India.

Cooperative aid to developing nations was given a broader context when the assistance agencies of the five Nordic countries joined in a project of training and education for Tanzania and later for Kenya. Their work was closely aligned with the cooperators who had pioneered in furthering cooperation in the Third World. The Danish agency DANIDA administers the project of the five Nordic nations.

This did not mean that assistance from cooperators stopped as government moved in. New premises for a Cooperative College in Tanzania were built with the help of funds from the Swedish Cooperative Center. Increasingly the SCC worked with the Swedish International Development Authority (SIDA), the government agency planning and administering all aid projects, in supporting cooperative development in a half-dozen countries. Cooperators are realistic about the amount of funds they contribute as compared to the volume that comes from SIDA. But they believe it is seed money that inspires the government agency to move on a much larger scale in assisting rapidly growing co-ops in the developing nations of Asia, Africa, and Latin America. The SCC continued to send experienced cooperators to help initiate centers in Africa. Arne Holmberg was named the first regional director of a center in northern Tanzania. He served until the post went to Dan Nyanjom, former cooperative commissioner in Kenya.

In writing the story of the Swedish and other national cooperative societies under the title "International Cooperation for Self-Reliance," Mauritz Bonow gives full

credit to what other cooperators have done. He cites the
example of the Cooperative League of the USA, which for
twenty years, working with the cooperative movement in
India, the Indian federal government, and the United
States AID agency, has greatly expanded the use of fertilizers so vital to raising the level of Indian food consumption. More than 25,000 cooperatives on various levels
across all India now control more than 50 percent of fertilizer distribution. The Indian Farmers' Fertilizer Cooperative (IFFCO) has an ammonia plant with a capacity of
910 tons per day and two other plants for different kinds
of fertilizer, each with a capacity of 1,200 tons.

Two other industrialized nations, Britain and the
Netherlands, have contributed credit assistance to help
meet balance of payments requirements. Increasingly the
emphasis in the cooperative movement in Sweden is on a
world without boundaries, that is, on international
cooperation, with the United Nations and its various
agencies high on the agenda. One of the most ardent expo-
nents of a world without boundaries is Nils Thedin. He
was for many years the chief information officer of KF and
in that capacity edited the magazine *Vi* (We), which went
to several hundred thousand Swedish cooperators.

In quite a different context Thedin has been in some
respects almost as important a figure as Albin Johansson.
This has been above all in turning what might have been
merely a big business organization, as its derogators like to
say, toward broader objectives both nationally and internationally. He has been an active participant in the work
of the United Nations International Children's Fund
(UNICEF). The Gutavsberg pottery works, a large-scale
enterprise that manufactures plumbing fixtures as well as
fine china, acquired by KF, makes small figurines repre-
senting many of the countries in UNICEF. Part of the pro-
ceeds from the sale of these figurines goes to UNICEF.

Slender, looking when I saw him in 1976 much
younger than his sixty-seven years, Thedin might be cata-

logued as an intellectual were it not for the practical drive he brings to the goals that are his principal concern. He has been chairman of UNICEF's executive council three times, a record for the organization of volunteers who contribute so much in time and effort to alleviating the hunger and homelessness of half the children of the world. Thedin remarked with quiet pride that Sweden is now contributing more to UNICEF than the United States.

A continuing concern of the Swedish Cooperative Center is the recruitment of able cooperators willing to break into their work in some aspect of the Swedish cooperative movement to go to a difficult post in a strange land on a leave of absence that may be as long as several years. This has meant uncertainty in the future career and financial security of the individual. According to a leaflet put out by SCC, these problems are under discussion, and the expectation is that in coming years cooperative organizations will be more and more liberal in extending leaves as well as in judging the value of having worked in foreign countries, so that no one will be cut off in the middle of his professional career. Swedish cooperators readily acknowledge that what they are doing in the developing world is a microcosm of the need. But it is a pledge of the hope and the idealism motivating thousands of men and women.

In so many ways Sweden has reached out to the world beyond its borders. In another way—through the immigration of workers—the outside world has touched one of the very foundations of Swedish life—the homogeneity of its people. One remarkable phenomenon of the boom years of the 1960s was the movement of millions seeking work in Germany, Switzerland, and France, where there was an acute labor shortage. They came from Italy, Turkey, Yugoslavia, and Greece, and the share of their earnings they sent home helped to bolster shaky economies. When the recession began and the need tapered off they were sent back. It was as though a piece of machinery which had become superfluous had been discarded.

It was not like that in Sweden, where there had also been a large influx of foreign labor. In the mid-1960s a lively debate began over the status of the immigrants. The consensus, typical of the reforms over forty years seeking social justice and equality of opportunity, was that the state had a responsibility which could not simply be ignored. Typical, too, was the appointment in 1968 of a Commission on Immigration to explore the whole question past and present. Out of the commission's extensive study came a statute giving Sweden a unique position in the postwar migrations. It was recognition of the reality of a profound change taking place—the transformation of one of the most homogeneous people to a multiethnic nation. The new law set three goals: equality between immigrants and Swedes, cultural freedom of choice for immigrants, and cooperation and solidarity between the native majority and the various ethnic minorities. With this went a number of specific reforms to implement the new policy.

transformation

The trade unions, working with immigration agencies of the government, insure that every immigrant worker receives the same benefits accorded a Swedish citizen. This means health and unemployment insurance, child support, free education, paid vacations, and the other fringe benefits. The immigrant is free to return to his homeland or to stay in Sweden and acquire citizenship after a period of five years, with immigrants from other Nordic countries becoming citizens in two years if they choose.

immigrant enjoys all the benefits

Of the approximately 1,100,000 immigrants in Sweden, 188,000 are Finish citizens; another 123,000 immigrants from Finland now have Swedish citizenship. Scandinavia today is a region without boundaries, so that citizens of Finland, Norway, Denmark, and Iceland may come and go as they choose. The large number of Finns is explained by an unemployment rate 20 to 30 percent higher than that in Sweden. The Danes are 32,000 of the immigrant total plus 28,000 who are citizens; the Norwegian figure is 27,000 plus 21,000. Next to the Nordic to-

tal the Yugoslavs account for 41,000 plus 8,000 who are citizens. Smaller numbers have come from Italy, Greece, Turkey, Germany, and Britain. In addition, 70,000-100,000 refugees from Hungary, Poland, and Estonia have settled in Sweden. The government appropriates more than $20 million annually for refugee work, much of it carried out through the United Nations High Commissioner for Refugees.

A determined effort has been made to give immigrants and their children a knowledge of their ethnic background. State grants go to national immigration organizations—Finnish, Yugoslav, Greek, Italian, and others—which have 80,000 members. Many of the reforms are directed toward immigrant children and are carried out through the schools to encourage them to take pride in and retain their mother tongue. Since 1977 every municipality is required to make available to immigrant children several hours of home language instruction at the preschool as well as at the basic compulsory school level. Lessons are being given to 30,000 pupils in fifteen different languages. Because children must ask for this instruction, consideration has been given to requiring immigrant children to take such courses. The annual cost is more than $40 million. The state is contributing to the production of literature in various minority languages and also making funds available for libraries to purchase foreign literature.

A law was passed in 1973 requiring employers to give their immigrant workers 240 hours of paid leave of absence to attend lessons in Swedish provided free of charge. Basic education is provided for illiterates, and more recently courses have been established through several universities and educational associations to train interpreters who, along with translators, are under state regulation. The first country in the world to have taken such a step, Sweden grants all aliens who have resided in the country for three years the right to vote in local elections and to hold local office. In 1976 220,000 aliens were entitled to

vote in the elections of that year, and 60 percent did so, while some 400 immigrants were elected to positions of public trust.

Recently Sweden's immigration policy has become more restrictive. Foreigners seeking employment in Sweden are required to obtain work permits through the Swedish consulate or embassy in the country in which they reside. It is difficult to obtain such permits. Foreign workers who become unemployed can have their labor permits extended and retain their right to stay in the country. The labor permit required before entering Sweden may be waived in certain cases, as when a spouse and minor child want to join an alien with a work permit already residing in Sweden. And these requirements naturally do not apply to refugees.

The program for immigrants illustrates the way in which Sweden has faced up to the profound change that is taking place. Today one out of every ten persons is either an immigrant or the offspring of an immigrant. Within a decade or two the ratio will be one out of three. The far-reaching and costly effort to integrate an alien people, while at the same time giving them the opportunity to preserve and cherish their ethnic identity, is proof, if proof were needed, of the continuity of the middle way. It reflects an inherent devotion to social justice and the common good.

But an incident that occurred at Södertälje, when young toughs attacked dark-skinned Assyrians working in a motor plant, shook the assumption of equality free of racial prejudice. The comfortable assurance of almost complete homogeneity had come to an end.

Equality of the sexes has not been challenged, however, and equal status for women ranks high among the goals of policy at home and abroad. In 1975 the U.N. General Assembly resolved that the International Women's Year should be followed by a Women's Decade, 1976-1985. Sweden had taken an influential part in the

World Conference of the International Women's Year. In Sweden itself, of the 349 members of the nation's unicameral legislature, 83 are women, and the number of women in gainful employment has long since passed the halfway mark. On Sweden's initiative the U.N. General Assembly decided that all the United Nations bodies concerned, the United Nations Development Program, and all specialized agencies should seek, each in its own field, to improve the status of women and periodically report to the General Assembly on the measures taken. With SIDA (the Swedish International Development Authority) proposing ways in the Swedish budget estimate for improving the lot of women in connection with Swedish aid programs, Ola Ullsten made this comment:

I regard the work in this field of vital importance mainly along the lines proposed by SIDA. In our cooperation with the program countries we have reason to emphasize the importance we attach to measures that improve the situation of women. At the same time we must stick to our view that measures for improving their status are an integrated part of the development we hope to support with our development assistance. In addition to measures coming within the country programs, funds should, in accordance with SIDA's proposal, be used both to support the work by women's organizations and to enable an active follow-up in international organizations of the action program adopted at the Conference of the International Women's Year in 1975.

So although neutral Sweden is allied to no military group, the role it plays in the world is an active one. Swedish intervention, Swedish strictures, are at times resented as mere busybodiness. But whether it is a Social Democratic government or a coalition of the right-of-center parties, this same involvement is likely to continue.

8   *The Future*

The nuclear accident in March 1979 at Three Mile Island
had profound consequences in Sweden. Widely publicized
in the Swedish press and on television, the accident was
devastating in its impact.

The dispute over nuclear energy which had been a
principal factor in the election of 1976 seemed, until
Three Mile Island, to have been resolved. It had ended
with a compromise on the nuclear option and safe disposal
of nuclear waste agreed to by the Social Democrats and
two parties, the Conservatives and the Liberals, that had
stood out in the coalition against Fälldin and his Center
party.

The compromise bill to be presented to the Riksdag
with certainty of passage contained the familiar call for
conservation of energy, measures to reduce Sweden's dependence on imported oil, and the promotion of extended
use of coal along with support for solar and wind energy.
Sweden was about to be the first government in the world
to announce its conviction that high-level waste could be
stored in an "absolutely safe way." This last was based on
complex storage containers to be placed in deep holes in
the granite substructure of the Swedish earth. Extensive
drilling had been done in the granite with one hole taken
to a depth of 500 meters, said to be large enough to store
waste from the entire Swedish nuclear program. A report
of the Nuclear Fuel Safety Commission set up by the
power industry found that the storage technique, with five
separate barriers against leakage, was safe enough, which

the government in the course of a prolonged political debate could take to mean "completely safe." Two nuclear
reactors, 7 and 8, which had stood idle for nearly a year,
could be fueled, and workmen could proceed with their
operation. Nuclear reactors 9 and 10 were already well
along toward completion, and 11 and 12 were to follow.

Three Mile Island put an abrupt end to this compromise. Having been the chief proponents of the nuclear
power program, the Social Democrats proposed a national
referendum on nuclear power in 1980. The six reactors
then in operation would continue, although one, the only
pressurized water reactor, was closed down for an overhaul
and would not resume operation for three months. Reactors 7 and 8 would not be fueled. A search for alternative
energy would commence, costing not less than $20 billion.
That was tentatively agreed to by the other parties.
Phrasing the questions for the referendum was no easy
task. The Center and the Communist parties were to form
the NO question, which would propose termination of all
nuclear power by 1990, with no more than six reactors to
be operated up to that year. YES would mean a vote for
the compromise energy bill, with twelve reactors providing nuclear energy into the indefinite future. The delay in
the national decision from 1979 to 1980 would cost an estimated $1 billion.

Other large questions about the future are still to be
answered. Remarkable advances in a welfare state have
been achieved peacefully and with the support of the great
majority. But as the heated debate over the Meidner plan
in the 1976 election campaign made clear, the concentration of the means of production in a relatively small number of private hands is bound to be increasingly an issue.
Will welfarism—what the critics on the left call "merely"
cradle-to-grave social insurance—suffice?

In a revised form of his plan, with the subtitle *Approach to Collective Capital Formation*, published in 1978 in
book form, Meidner describes the concentration of owner-

ship in the share capital of private corporations. In a study
Meidner directed of sixty-three companies it was shown that 1.5 percent of all private shareholders held as much as 34 percent of all shares privately held. In his conclusion he writes:

> As regards ownership the Swedish economy is scarcely a mixed economy at all; much more than most European economies, it is dominated by private ownership and there has been no appreciable change in this situation for many years. In respect of planning there has on the other hand been a sustained movement towards greater social influence over the economy.

If anything does typify the Swedish economy it is surely the mixture of an extremely modest degree of social ownership and a soaring ambition with regard to social influence over the course of economic events. This combination of private ownership and social control over the economy can in fact be said to constitute the foundation of the Swedish variation on the theme of the mixed economy.

Uncertainty over the course Sweden should take was reflected in the results of the September 1979 election. The Social Democratic party remained the largest party, with 154 members in the Riksdag, but its parliamentary alliance with the Communists, who won 22 seats, gave it one vote less than the three right-of-center parties, which won a total of 175 seats and therefore were charged with forming a government.

The campaign had been curiously muted. Palme took a cautious line on the Meidner plan, saying that no serious consideration could be given to it until 1981. He advocated a new production tax on business. The leader of the Conservative party, Gosta Bohman, conducted the only vigorous campaign, calling loud and clear for a reduction of taxes and a slowdown in the rate of increase in social benefits, though dismantling the welfare system was far from his intention. The Conservatives made the largest gain of any party.

The right-of-center parties managed to form a government, with Fälldin as prime minister, but how could a government with a majority of one take the difficult decisions ahead? The sheep farmer would have a perilous course with survival of his government likely to be on the line week after week.

The dilemma Sweden presents today has significance far beyond the borders of this small country in the north of Europe. It poses a question that has a larger meaning for a world troubled by confusion and conflict, a meaning that is as much philosophic as it is economic. One way to put it is to ask whether a welfare system—cradle-to-the-grave security—as comprehensive as it is in Sweden can be sustained in a society where the means of production are so narrowly held. Or does the existence of a privileged owning class make the full step to socialism inevitable in a democratic state?

The answers are many and varied. With the level of taxation so high as to have reached almost the point of confiscation, the privileged feel that the rewards of ownership have been reduced close to the vanishing point. Swedish industrialists have long been creative and innovative, which is one reason for an export market that has competed successfully with far larger economies as in Germany and Britain. But they are beginning to feel that laws such as that governing decisions in the work place are so inhibiting and time-consuming as to be a brake on innovative production.

The question of equality enters in. Is it to be an egalitarian society with neither highs nor lows in the distribution of goods and services—a smooth, well-ordered mean, look-alikes in housing, clothes, every aspect of life? That has not been true in the past, and the dreary example of the egalitarianism of Eastern Europe is close at hand as a warning. Here is a well-paid worker at a Volvo plant, with a car and a small boat. But here is a highly successful industrialist, say Curt Nicolin of ASEA, with a sailing yacht three or four times the size and range of the worker's boat,

and with auxiliary motors. Is this to be evened out in the
years ahead by ever higher taxation on ownership? Is that
to be the direction of the Social Democrats under the pressure of Meidner and the left wing of the party? I believe
the answer is in the negative. For however much the Swedish people may value evenhanded fair play, equality of opportunity, and an old age without poverty, they have long
appreciated the graces, the adornments, that raise the level
of living above merely meat and potatoes.

But what might be called the fact of involuntary socialism is part of the dilemma. The three bourgeois parties,
during the brief time of their coalition, socialized more
of the economy than the Social Democrats ever did. They
did this by intervening to put the state in a substantial position of ownership in major industries—steel, mining, shipbuilding—primarily to save these industries from bank-
ruptcy under the impact of the recession and the decline of
the export market. It was done, too, to shift the responsibility for the jobs of those who would otherwise be thrown
out of work onto public make-work. This is hardly the socialism of Marx and Engels. It was state intervention under
dire necessity. Whether these industries can be restored to
profitability with a reduction in thousands of jobs depends
as much on the world market as it does on the economy of
Sweden. The final answer to the dilemma of equality will
not come from Sweden. But the decisions taken by a
highly conscientious electorate will be illuminating for the
industrialized, unionized West.

The reforms of the middle way have been far-reaching
and costly. In slicing the economic pie, little is left for in- *little for*
vestment funds essential to industrial development and the *investment—*
competitive position of the Swedish economy. This is a *dn't funds*
point made repeatedly by men of finance and industry.
But it is also raised by Meidner and the executive council
of the Labor Organisationen as buttressing the logic of employee funds accrued out of company profits and thereby
available for investment.

One thing can be said for certain. The process of

change in Sweden is slow and deliberate. What has been done over nearly five decades cannot be abruptly undone. Nevertheless, the direction to be taken in the immediate future will say a great deal about the resolution of the dilemma of a social system that has taken such long strides down the road of welfarism.

Bibliography

Ames, J. W. *Without Boundaries: Co-operative Sweden Today and Tomorrow*. Great Britain, The Co-Operative Union Ltd., 1971.

Andersson, Ingvar, and Weibull, Jörgen. *Swedish History in Brief*. Stockholm, The Swedish Institute, 1973.

Bonow, Mauritz. *International Co-operation for Self-Reliance*. Stockholm, Swedish Cooperative Center, 1975.

Cerny, Karl H., ed. *Scandinavia at the Polls*. Washington, D.C., American Enterprise Institute for Public Policy Research, 1977.

Haagerup, Niels Jörgen. *A Brief Introduction to Danish Foreign Policy and Defence*. Denmark, Ministry of Defense, 1975.

Jenkins, David. *Sweden and the Price of Progress*. New York, Coward-McCann, 1968.

Koblik, Steven, ed. *Sweden's Development from Poverty to Affluence, 1750 to 1970*. Minneapolis, University of Minnesota Press, 1975.

Lindbeck, Assar. *Swedish Economic Policy*. Berkeley, University of California Press, 1974.

Lundberg, W. T. *Consumer Owned: Sweden's Cooperative Democracy*. Palo Alto, Calif., Consumers Cooperative Publishing Association, 1978.

Meidner, Rudolf, and Uhman, Berndt. *Fifteen Years of Wage Policy*. Stockholm, Swedish Trade Union Confederation, 1972.

Myrdal, Alva. *The Game of Disarmament*. New York, Pantheon, 1977.

Nicolin, Curt. *Private Industry in a Public World*. Reading, Mass., Addison-Wesley Publishing Co., 1977.

Swedish Council for Information on Alcohol and Other Drugs. *The Alcohol Question in Sweden, A Survey*. Stockholm, n.d.

Swedish Ministry of Labor. *Towards Democracy in the Work Place*. Stockholm, January 1977.

Index